CONFRONTATIONS

CONFRONTATIONS
Studies in Irish History

J. C. Beckett

FABER & FABER
3 Queen Square, London

First published in 1972
by Faber and Faber Limited
3 Queen Square, London WC1
Printed in Great Britain by
Latimer Trend & Co Ltd Plymouth
All rights reserved

ISBN 0 571 09960 2

© *J. C. Beckett 1972*

Contents

PREFACE   *page* 9

1. THE STUDY OF IRISH HISTORY: AN INAUGURAL
   LECTURE
   (Queen's University, Belfast. 1963)   11

2. IRISH-SCOTTISH RELATIONS IN THE SEVEN-
   TEENTH CENTURY
   (*Transactions of the Belfast Natural History and
   Philosophical Society*, 1964)   26

3. THE CONFEDERATION OF KILKENNY REVIEWED
   (*Historical studies II*, ed. M. Roberts. Bowes &
   Bowes, Cambridge. 1959)   47

4. THE IRISH VICEROYALTY IN THE RESTORATION
   PERIOD
   (*Transactions of the Royal Historical Society*,
   5th series, vol. 20. 1970)   67

5. THE GOVERNMENT AND THE CHURCH OF IRE-
   LAND UNDER WILLIAM III AND ANNE
   (*Irish historical studies*, ii, no. 7. 1941) 87

6. SWIFT: THE PRIEST IN POLITICS   111

7. ANGLO-IRISH CONSTITUTIONAL RELATIONS
   IN THE LATER EIGHTEENTH CENTURY
   (*Irish historical studies*, xiv, no. 53. 1964) 123

8. IRELAND UNDER THE UNION
   (*Topic: 13*, Washington, Pennsylvania. 1967) 142

9. THE CHURCH OF IRELAND: DISESTABLISHMENT
   AND ITS AFTERMATH
   (*Theology*, lxxiii, no. 599. 1970)   *page* 152

10. CARSON—UNIONIST AND REBEL
    (*Leaders and men of the Easter rising: Dublin
    1916*, ed. F. X. Martin, Methuen & Co.,
    London. 1967)   160

INDEX OF NAMES   171

Preface

OF the ten essays that make up this volume nine have already been published, and they reappear here with only minor alterations. The date and place of original publication are indicated in the table of contents. The essay on Swift is now printed for the first time.

Though the volume ranges over several centuries and a variety of topics, it is concerned throughout, in one way or another, with those elements of conflict that have played such a large part in Ireland's past and have left a troublesome legacy to the present generation. It is, at least in part, because these conflicts do not fit readily into a clear pattern of development that the writing of a history of Ireland over any extended period presents special difficulties. These difficulties form the theme of the first essay; and the others, if they accomplish nothing else, may at least serve to illustrate the problems there discussed.

Queen's University   J. C. BECKETT
Belfast
September 1971

One

The Study of Irish History: An Inaugural Lecture

IN 1689 Sir Richard Cox published in London the first volume of
a history of Ireland, entitled *Hibernia Anglicana*, and prefaced
it by an explanatory address to the reader, of which this is the
opening paragraph:

> Since Ireland is reckoned among the principal islands of the
> world, and deserves to be esteemed so (whether you consider the
> situation of the country, the number and goodness of its har-
> bours, the fruitfulness of the soil, or the temperature of the
> climate); it is strange that this noble kingdom, and the affairs of
> it, should find no room in history, but remain so very obscure,
> that not only the inhabitants know little or nothing of what has
> passed in their own country; but even England, a learned and
> inquisitive nation, skilful beyond comparison in the histories of all
> other countries, is nevertheless but very imperfectly informed in
> the story of Ireland, though it be a kingdom subordinate to
> England and of the highest importance to it.

The rest of Sir Richard Cox's address is taken up with strictures
on his predecessors and with justification of his own work, and it
is not my intention to follow his example in either respect. But
the passage that I have quoted still retains, after almost three
centuries, an uncomfortable degree of truth. The deficiency in
knowledge of matters of fact has, indeed, very largely been made
good. The antiquarian researches of the seventeenth century
were continued and expanded in the eighteenth. With the nineteenth century came the systematic publication of source material,
which has continued to the present day. And the past generation
or so has seen a whole series of specialist monographs, which, if
not exactly illustrating (to adapt the words of Scott's Antiquary)
'all that is clear, and all that is dark, and all that is neither dark
nor clear, but hovers in the dusky twilight in the region of

Hibernian antiquities', have at least solved many outstanding problems in Irish history, as well (perhaps) as a few that were not recognized as problems until their solutions were presented. With all this material at our disposal, we have now little excuse for being ignorant of the events that have passed in our country. But knowledge is not understanding. A succession of events is not a history. And a succession of 'problems', though discussed with all the critical apparatus of modern historical scholarship, cannot provide a pattern of development. We may, in one sense, know what happened; but do we know what Irish history is about?

Before enlarging on this, it may perhaps be well to comment on the wider implications of the question. What, we may ask, is history itself about? To this question, taken in its most absolute form, there is no strictly historical answer—except that, simply as historians, we do not know. Those who attempt, as well as they can, to survey the field of world history, to take in at one sweep the whole of the recorded and recoverable past of mankind, may profess to find in it some recognizable theme, and may reduce it to a pattern, or a series of patterns. But in fact these patterns are imposed from without; they are derived from theological or metaphysical premises, which history may or may not support, but which it cannot itself supply. But though world history has long been a popular exercise, most historians have, in practice, confined themselves within more manageable boundaries, both of space and time; and in particular they have tended to concentrate on what one may for convenience call 'national history'—that is, the history of a particular group in relation to a particular territory. Working within such limits, it is possible for the historian to find a pattern rather than to impose it—to elicit it from the facts, not to twist the facts to suit it. And a pattern thus honestly come by is the answer to the question: What is this particular piece of history about? The answer is, of course, partial and incomplete, and its validity is only relative; but in so far as the historian has been able to deal honestly with his material, it is a strictly historical answer, and independent of political or theological or metaphysical influences. It is this kind of answer—this pattern of development—that I find difficulty in eliciting from the facts of Irish history.

One possible (or, rather, inevitable) comment will be that the pattern is in fact there, plain for all to see, if I did not blindly, or wilfully, overlook it; and to this comment I shall return later. But there is another kind of comment that may also be made, and that had better be dealt with now. Irish history (it may be argued) is not of any great importance; no country, one historian (the late Eli Heckscher) has said, has a right to expect that its history should be studied just because it has happened; and if the history of Ireland is so difficult to understand might not historians employ their time better in some other field? Now we must certainly admit that there is a hierarchy of importance in national histories—the history of France is more important to Europe, and to the world, than the history of Norway. But the history of any country must be of importance, as well as of interest, to the people who live there; and the greater the difficulty in understanding it, the more important it is that it should be studied. For only by understanding the past can we enter into a free relationship with it; only then can tradition, precedent, and example—good guides, but bad drivers—exercise their legitimate and beneficent influence. I believe that Irish history has significance beyond Ireland; but even if this is not so, we in this country cannot safely refuse to make an honest attempt to understand our own past.

One difficulty, and perhaps the fundamental difficulty, that besets us in making this attempt can most clearly be shown by comparing Ireland with England. As early as the eleventh century the future course of English history was already determined in two vital respects: from that time onwards the unity and the independence of the country were secure. There was one centre of authority, though it might be more or less effective in different parts of the country; and if this central authority was sometimes in the hands of men who were not themselves of English birth, it was at least always English by situation and interest. There were occasional civil wars, which might sometimes appear to have a regional basis; but they were always struggles for the control of the central authority, never attempts to break up the unity of the kingdom. Thus the student of English history finds outlined for him a ready-made pattern, inherent in the subject itself. Whether his prime interest is in politics or administration, in constitutional development or economic expansion, in social legislation, in the arts, or in the church, his material has a natural and overriding unity, which binds even the most apparently diverse elements in a common relationship. More than this, all these elements in English history, and all those others that I have not mentioned, are linked one to another in a relationship that is basically and essentially English. Together, they make up the history of a society, which might indeed, if seen in isolation, appear to be infinitely divided, but which, seen in its European and world setting, has a separate and unified existence of its own.

No doubt I have over-simplified the course and character of English history; and the experts could, if they thought it worth while, correct me on many points of detail. But my essential contention would remain—that there is in English history a natural and recognizable pattern, even if that pattern is slightly more complicated or slightly less regular than I have represented it.

Contrast this with the confusion, the cross-currents, the apparent inconsequence of events, the regional isolationism, that meet the student of Irish history. Where is he to begin? Where is he to place his centre of interest? Where, above all, is he to find a theme that will lead him, by some process of development, from one era to the next?

The historian of England, one might say, is like a traveller making a journey through a well-mapped country. He may venture into little-trodden by-ways, or even leave the path altogether for the open countryside. But he is never far from a known route; and though he may sometimes be in doubt about his actual position on the map, he can place it within narrow limits. And he can always find his way home. He may, if he is fortunate, discover new relations between one district and another, he may suggest new and useful lines of communication, he may reveal unsuspected wealth in areas hitherto despised or ignored. From time to time more adventurous explorers (the Touts, the Namiers, and their disciples) may raise excited cries, demanding that the whole map must be re-drawn in the light of their discoveries. But when the excitement has died down, all that is found necessary is to alter the height of a hill or two, or retrace the course of a tributary stream. The coasts stand impregnable; mountain and plain, river and lake, keep their old positions; and though the colouring of the landscape may vary with seed-time and harvest, the landscape itself remains recognizably the same.

It would be misleading to suggest that the Irish historian sets out into an unknown wilderness. Many of the areas through which he must travel have already been carefully charted. But there is no general agreement as to how the charts are to be fitted together, or how they should stand in relation to areas as yet imperfectly known. There are many well-marked roads, but often they seem to lead from nowhere to nowhere, and they do not provide a continuous route. Worst of all, there is doubt about the limits of the area he is to explore. He has not only to undertake a journey into the interior, he has also to demarcate the frontiers. In making such a journey, the traveller must be fortified against disappointment: he can hardly define his goal until he has attained it, and he is more than likely to lose himself on the way.

The difficulty, thus allegorically represented, in writing the history of Ireland is not, it seems to me, a very serious one in relation to the pre-Norman period. This statement may appear strange to those who have found themselves bewildered by the conflicting views of the experts, who have wrestled with MacNeill, who have lost sleep over O'Rahilly, and who have felt the firm earth crumble beneath them as they saw the patriarchal figure of St Patrick dissolve into a goodly fellowship of prophets. But, in fact, Irish history down to the twelfth century has a self-contained and continuing character of its own, a character that will survive, whatever view we take of the high kingship, or whichever side we espouse in the unending wars of the linguists. We can find in this period a pattern of development, vague and incomplete, but discernible; and it is the interruption of this development by the arrival of the Anglo-Normans that throws over the history of the succeeding centuries an air of seemingly hopeless confusion.

It is, I imagine, at this point that those who would attribute my difficulty in understanding Irish history merely to the blindness of prejudice will have their own explanatory pattern ready. For them, the history of Ireland from the twelfth century to the twentieth is a long-drawn-out war between the Gael and the Gall, the unremitting struggle of an inextinguishable nation to repel the invader. And this interpretation can find some appearance of support in the events of the present century. The Gaelic Revival, the revolution of 1912–23, the establishment of an Irish republic, committed to a Gaelic cultural policy, might be taken to indicate the goal towards which all Irish history has been moving since the time of Henry II. But the writing of history can never be simply teleological; it is influenced, but not governed, by the end to which it moves; the process is more important than the conclusion. And to find any process of historical development that connects resistance to the Anglo-Normans in the twelfth century with resistance to the Black-and-Tans in the twentieth, one must not only ignore the evidence that does exist, but invent evidence that does not exist. Dr. Michael Tierney has summed up this interpretation, and its weakness, very cogently:

> A very popular way of looking at our history is to conceive of it as having been guided in all its phases by one true doctrine, the doctrine of nationality, all other explanations being dismissed as aberrant. This one true doctrine is often believed to be of immortal native origin and is evoked with equal rigour to explain the course of events in the twelfth, the seventeenth, or the nineteenth century. Thus construed and invoked, it makes nonsense of a great part of our history; for in this rigid form it is a product of the late eighteenth century and was first popularly preached only a little more than a hundred years ago.[1]

It is easy to dismiss the interpretation here condemned as a figment of national pride, or an instrument of political propaganda; but we must consider it also in another, and more respectable, character; for it is an attempt to answer the question with which we began: what is Irish history about? The answer is naïvely unhistorical; but its very failure to satisfy us as historians serves to throw into relief the problem with which we are faced. It is just because the innumerable conflicts, military and political, that fill the records of Irish history do *not* represent the repeated confrontation of recognizable opposing forces, that it appears so nearly impossible to link them to any idea of progress or recession on a national scale.

When we look at Ireland in the middle of the sixteenth century, 400 years after the establishment of Henry II's lordship, and try to make any sort of historical sense out of the intervening period, we are almost driven to the desperate expedient of a negative interpretation, to consider rather what might have happened than what actually did happen. The Anglo-Normans might have completed their conquest, and established a strong feudal state; but though they followed up their first successes with daring enterprise, and penetrated to the extremities of the country, north and west and south, their resources soon became exhausted and their power declined. The Irish kings, faced with a common danger, might have united to recover the whole island; but traditional jealousies and quarrels proved too strong, their alliances were unstable and short-lived, and each man was content to fight for his own hand. The English monarchy's neglect of Ireland, and the gradual mingling of Norman with Gael, might have tempted some strong-minded leader to establish for himself an independent kingdom, attracting the united allegiance of both races; but the one man who came near to doing so, the Great Earl of Kildare, had no ambition to be more than a royal deputy, and the unrivalled power that he established at the end of the fifteenth century was overthrown in the next generation. One might say, with little exaggeration, that the history of medieval Ireland is a record of broken-off developments.

It is, of course, the business of the historian to trace these developments as far as they go, and to explain (if he can) why they go no farther. But in doing so, he finds himself faced with a double problem. There is, first, the problem of unity. Once we go beyond such general statements as I have just been making about medieval Ireland, the history of the period tends to fall apart into a series of regional histories; for we are dealing not with one power centre or with one community, but with many and the political relations between them were often not much closer than those between the European states of the nineteenth century. And if we seek for unity by treating all the various regions in relation to the royal government in Dublin, we at once come up against another problem, more intractable and more enduring than the first. Careless as English kings usually were of their Irish lordship, they maintained some contact with their representatives here, and some control over policy. Dublin, the capital of the lordship, was, in appearance almost wholly, in population very largely, an English city. If, therefore, we are to look at medieval Ireland through the eyes of Dublin, we may find ourselves studying, not so much the history of Ireland, as a subdivision of the history of England.

This point becomes of crucial importance from the seventeenth century onwards. By then, Ireland had been politically unified; for the last years of Elizabeth had seen a complete and systematic conquest. Now, for the first time, there was one central authority, effective throughout the whole country, and one system of law, universally administered by royal judges. But the central authority

B

was that of the English monarchy, and was exercised in accordance with English policy; the law was the common law of England, and cases could be called, on appeal, from Irish to English courts. We may, indeed, speak of the 'Kingdom of Ireland' as a politically unified area, with its own constitution, its own administrative and legal systems, its own government; but this kingdom was like a clock whose face was in Ireland, while the works were in England. The historian's problem has been modified, but not fundamentally changed.

It may be said that a very similar problem must arise, more or less acutely, in writing the history of any dependent country—the history of Norway from the Union of Kalmar to 1905, the history of Bohemia and Hungary under the Hapsburgs. But a vital distinction must be made. Each of these countries had already, while still independent, established a national identity, expressing itself in political institutions; and these institutions, surviving in some form under foreign rule, helped to maintain the continuity of national life. In Ireland, the only political institutions surviving from pre-Norman times were local not national; their influence, until they finally disappeared in the seventeenth century, tended to divide rather than unite the country; and the political institutions by which Ireland was actually governed, from the seventeenth century onwards, were imported from outside and they were managed by colonists. This brings us to another, and even more important, characteristic of the Irish situation. The influx of settlers from England produced a sharply divided population. In course of time, the original racial division was partly obscured and partly accentuated by religious controversy; and by the end of the seventeenth century the division had become one of religion rather than of race. But the division itself has remained, to confuse and complicate almost every issue with which the historian of Ireland has to deal. The very term 'Irish' itself becomes one of doubtful significance. It may, according to the context (or according to the taste and fancy of the writer) stand for the whole population of Ireland; or for those of Gaelic descent, as opposed to the colonists, or for the Roman Catholics, as opposed to the protestants, without regard to descent; or for the colonists (English by blood but Irish by birth), as opposed to more recent arrivals. Such ambiguity sometimes opens the way for historical legerdemain. Sir Jonah Barrington's

Rise and fall of the Irish nation, published in 1833, is concerned
solely with the fortunes of that small section of the population,
wholly English in language, and very largely English by descent,
which exercised a quasi-independent control over the government of Ireland for a brief period at the end of the eighteenth
century; but in the first page of the book the author, passing
rapidly from the age of Henry II to the age of the American
Revolution, calmly assumes that the 'Irish nation' about which
he is writing is the natural and logical successor of the 'Irish
nation' of the twelfth century. There may, perhaps, be something
to say for this point of view; but it is certainly not the self-evident
truth that Barrington makes it appear.

For the historian who rejects Barrington's easy equivalence of
one age with another, who is not content to use terms without
examining them, and who doubts his power to create a nation by
a stroke of the pen, the study of Irish history must (as I hope I
have shown) present a formidable problem. So long as he confines himself within the narrow boundaries of specialist research
he may avoid or even ignore it. But if he is rash enough to venture
on a general history of Ireland over any extended period he is
forced to recognize (if he takes what he is doing at all seriously)
that his position is very different from that of the historian of
England or of France, that the boundaries of his subject are ill-
defined, that its theme is uncertain, and that that degree of self-
contained continuity and relative independence, which most
obviously justifies separate historical treatment, seems sometimes
to be lacking. How, in these circumstances, should the historian
of Ireland set about his task? I shall consider the question with
special reference to the period since the seventeenth century;
for it is in dealing with this period that the problem I have described is most acute, and the temptation to leave it on one side
most pressing.

Three kinds of answer to the question suggest themselves:
(1) It may be argued that the historian of any country must be
concerned, in the first place, with those whose actions and attitudes had a direct and decisive effect on its condition; and that
since for more than three centuries every important decision
respecting the government of Ireland was taken in England, it is
impossible to give any intelligible account of the course of events
in this country save in relation to English politics. Just as the

constitutional lawyers held Ireland to be a kingdom 'inseparately annexed and subordinate unto the crown of England', so the history of Ireland, though presenting local variations and peculiarities, might be regarded as annexed and subordinate to the history of England. It is worth noting that one of the greatest of Irish historians, W. E. H. Lecky, planned his *History of Ireland in the eighteenth century*, not as a distinct work, but as part of his *History of England in the eighteenth century*.

(2) The same line of argument may result in a totally different attitude. For (it may be said) if the history of Irish government is really English history, then the historian of Ireland must be concerned with something else; and he will find his themes in those spheres of life lying most remote from government control, and in the activities of those who resisted its authority—in literature, in folklore, in agrarian agitation and revolutionary conspiracy.

(3) The historian may confine his attention to events and developments in Ireland, taking things, so to speak, as he finds them. Thus he will simply accept the overriding power of the English government as a limiting factor in Irish politics, much as one might recognize the influence of the weather on a battle, without detailed examination of the climatic conditions that produced it.

I am not suggesting that any Irish historian could be placed precisely in one of these three categories. But there are these attitudes of mind; and in any work on Irish history involving the review of an extended period one or other tends to prevail. It must be made clear that we are not here concerned simply with variety of interpretation, to which the history of any country must be liable. It is not a matter of comparing different versions of the same narrative, of trying to reconcile whig and tory, marxist and non-marxist, or even nationalist and unionist. The problem is the far more fundamental one of trying to define the subject matter with which any historian of Ireland, whatever his political colour, ought to be concerned.

Each of the three attitudes I have described seems to me to be unsatisfactory, or even dangerous; for each, though not in the same way or to the same extent, tends to produce a distorted or unbalanced view of the past. The danger can be illustrated even from such a brilliant work as Lecky's *Ireland in the eighteenth century*. Lecky is so much concerned to trace government policy to its true source in England, that the book is not so much a history of Ireland as a history of Anglo-Irish relations; and the political events and developments that receive fullest attention are those in which the interests of the British ministry were directly involved. Furthermore, the same attitude has affected his treatment of other, non-political, aspects of Irish life. Whereas in his *History of England in the eighteenth century* he examines at great length the development and variety of religious opinion, in the *History of Ireland* these topics are cursorily dismissed, except where they have some political significance. John Wesley, for example, makes a great figure in Lecky's account of eighteenth-century England; but if we were to judge Wesley's Irish importance solely from the pages of Lecky we might pardonably suppose that it lay mainly in the fact that his diary contains some acute and quotable comments on the state of the country.

If there is some danger in thus linking Irish history too closely to British, there is even more in concentrating solely on events in Ireland. Whether the historian rejects the whole governmental system as a foreign imposition, and finds his themes elsewhere; or accepts it as part of the Irish scene, without any detailed investigation of its British background, he is bound to misrepresent the past. Irish history so written has an appearance of spontaneity and independence that is, in fact, spurious; events, explained in purely Irish terms, are given a false emphasis; both Irish achievements and Irish grievances are exaggerated. Rather paradoxically, the influence of Great Britain tends to play a disproportionately large part in this kind of Irish history: accepted, without being examined, and commonly personified simply as 'England', it can be used to explain every misfortune, political or economic, from which Ireland has ever suffered. No one could deny that British misunderstanding and mishandling of Irish affairs have often had unhappy consequences for Ireland, and it is not the historian's business to palliate or justify the conduct of governments; but it is his business to present it, as fairly as he can, in the light of all the relevant circumstances. And so we come full circle: for if the historian is obliged to consider British policy towards Ireland in all its aspects, he can hardly avoid the close linking up of British and Irish history that I have just criticized as unsatisfactory and dangerous.

At this stage, then, the argument seems to have led us to an inescapable dilemma, to the conclusion that the history of Ireland, however it is written, must suffer either distortion by being treated on its own, or extinction by being submerged in the history of Great Britain. But this destructive argument has been a necessary preparation for what I take to be my real task here—that is, to explain the distinctive function of the historian of Ireland. All that I have said so far has been designed to show that the phrase 'history of Ireland' is not, despite similarity of form, susceptible of the same relatively simple interpretation as the phrases 'history of England', 'history of France'. And even if we bring into comparison the much more complicated histories of Germany and Italy, we can find in either a more easily recognizable pattern of unity and continuity than in the history of Ireland.

To some people it may seem that this anxiety to find a pattern is quite unreasonable, and that the student of Irish history can get on comfortably without it. He can select his topic, define his problem, delimit his boundaries in advance, and then devote himself to his research untroubled by the difficulties that I have been describing, or, some might say, inventing. Nothing could be farther from my mind than even to appear to disparage work done in this way, the more we have of it the better. But if it is to make its full contribution to our understanding of the past there must be some framework of reference into which it can fall, and which it may, from time to time, modify. It is the need for such a framework that justifies the attempt to write not just Irish history but the history of Ireland.

The argument put forward in the earlier part of this lecture might appear to suggest (as I have hinted already) that the history of Ireland cannot, in fact, be written in any satisfactory manner. But to conclude thus would be to overlook an assumption implicit in the discussion at that stage—the assumption, that is, that if the history of Ireland can at all be written as a distinct and (relatively speaking) self-contained history, it must follow the same sort of unitary scheme as the history of England. On that assumption, it would certainly be true (if my reasoning is correct) that no satisfactory framework for such a history could be found. But must this assumption be accepted? Can we not find some other, and more hopeful line of approach?

What follows now is, of necessity, tentative. I do not think that the history of Ireland has yet been satisfactorily written; and I am not so bold as to suppose either that I myself am likely to succeed where better scholars have failed, or that I can point out infallibly the path to be taken. But I can put forward some suggestions, which, if they serve no other purpose, may at least indicate grounds for believing that the problem I have stated need not be insoluble.

The history of Ireland, like the history of any other country, must be based on a study of the relationship between the land and the people—the people, that is, not just as exploiters of the natural resources, but the people considered politically, using that word in its widest sense. But at no time between the twelfth century and the twentieth can we speak of the people of Ireland as a single political community—at one time or another, groups of different cultural traditions have exercised varying degrees of control over the whole or part of the island, in more or less direct subordination to the external power of England. We have, therefore, an element of stability—the land, and an element of instability—the people. It is to the stable element that we must look for continuity. The historian of England may entitle his work, at choice, 'The history of England', or 'The history of the English people', and no one expects a difference of title to indicate a difference of content—the terms are interchangeable. But the historian of Ireland must write, specifically, 'The history of *Ireland*'; for it is in Ireland itself, the physical conditions imposed by life in this country, and their effect on those who have lived here, that he will find the distinct and continuing character of Irish history. For this reason, he will be no less concerned with the settlers who have established themselves here, at any time since the twelfth century, than with the pre-Norman population. To the Gaelic nationalist, the settlers may remain foreign invaders, an English garrison; but to the historian they are as much part of the Irish scene as the lands they conquered, the castles they built, the institutions they imported or devised.

The settlers never formed a single, continuing element in the population. They arrived here at intervals, so that we can distinguish between one layer of settlement and another, as well as between settlements from England and settlements from Scotland. Some mingled readily with the native population, some kept themselves apart. But all were subjected to the same physical influences of life in Ireland, and also to the same social influences which, whether working by repulsion or attraction, affected even those who had no tincture of Gaelic blood. The outlook and traditions they had brought with them were gradually modified; and though they did not wholly cease to be English or Scottish, they became in time Anglo-Irish or (to use an American term) Scotch-Irish.

These divisions among the settlers provide one reason, among others, why the history of Ireland cannot be reduced to a simple struggle between native and foreigner, or written on the same sort of unitary scheme as the history of England. On a broad view, the historian will necessarily be concerned with the whole population; but at different times different groups will occupy the centre of the stage. He must free himself from the notion that he can treat any one of them, any single political community, as his permanent theme. He must be prepared, that is, for an element of discontinuity. But once he has accepted this, he will find that amid the fluctuating conflicts of these unstable groups there is also an element of continuity—the influence of the land itself. And he must consider not only what this influence achieved, but what it failed to achieve; not only where it advanced, but where it was driven back. The former may seem straightforward and commonplace—every schoolboy has been told that the Norman settlers became *Hiberniciores Hibernicis ipsis*. The historian, however, cannot be satisfied with generalizations, and must examine in more detail in what, precisely, the 'Irishness' of the Anglo-Irish consisted. And this inquiry will bring him, if not directly yet inevitably, to the second consideration: a large proportion of the settlers resisted complete surrender to the influence of Ireland, and the traditions, ideas, and institutions they had imported not only survived, though in modified form, but profoundly affected the earlier population. Sometimes they were freely accepted, more often they were imposed by force; but however they operated, the effect was the same; and among the whole Gaelic population a way of life that had been produced by Irish conditions was challenged, and in some measure submerged, by a way of life that had grown up in Britain. This is a development that has sometimes been neglected, though the evidence of its importance stares us in the face: the whole population, whatever its racial origin, has been continuously subjected, from the seventeenth century to the present day, to a political and administrative organization, and to a legal system, that had their origins in Great Britain.

The stress here laid on the settler element in the population must not be interpreted to mean that our history should simply embody an Anglo-Irish tradition; the history of that tradition is, in fact, at once narrower and wider than the history of Ireland. But it is by studying the way in which the settlers were influenced by the conditions of Irish life, and the way in which they themselves modified the influence of those conditions on the earlier population, that we may be able to identify the distinctive characteristics of Irish history, and build up a framework round which that history may be written. I do not say that the task will be easy, or that all the difficulties I have described in the earlier part of this lecture will be solved or circumvented. I do not know what kind of 'History of Ireland' will eventually emerge. What I am suggesting, after all, is not a programme of work, but a line of approach, an attitude of mind, a way of looking at the Irish past. What results from all this must be a matter for experiment, repeated, tedious, and laborious. But it is an experiment that we must have the patience, and the courage, to make.

NOTE

1. Michael Tierney, ed. *Daniel O'Connell: nine centenary essays.* Dublin, 1949, p. 151.

Two

Irish-Scottish Relations in the Seventeenth Century

THE long and close connection between Irish and Scottish history has its basis in geography. The North Channel is sometimes rough and occasionally dangerous; but the crossing is short enough to be practicable for open boats, and from the earliest times there has been easy and frequent intercourse between the two countries. The influence of this geographical factor has expressed itself in various ways, according to the political conditions prevailing in the British Isles as a whole. During the medieval period these conditions were fluctuating and uncertain; but Scottish involvement in Ireland tended to increase; and from the thirteenth century onwards heavy-armed footmen from the Western Isles, the gallowglasses, played a major part in Irish warfare—they were, says Curtis, 'the one part of an Irish army which could be trusted to stand its ground to the end'. The Bruces' attempt to bring all Ireland permanently under Scottish influence ended in failure, when Edward Bruce was defeated and killed at the battle of Faughart (1318); but Scottish monarchs continued to keep an eye on Irish affairs and occasionally tried to turn them to their own advantage. Even the cautious James VI maintained secret relations with Hugh O'Neill while he was in rebellion against Elizabeth.

The internal political condition of Scotland itself was in one respect not dissimilar from that of Ireland in the sixteenth century. For in Scotland also there was an almost continuous struggle between a centralizing royal government and the local independence of Gaelic chieftains, whose cultural tradition and political organization had close links with the native Irish. It is a matter of some significance that the part of Ireland in which Gaelic power lasted longest was the province of Ulster, which could most easily maintain intercourse with the western high-lands and islands of Scotland. Down to the end of the sixteenth century the history of Irish-Scottish relations is very largely concerned with the politics of the 'Celtic fringe'—with family and clan rivalries, and with the defence of local independence against central authority.

The opening of the seventeenth century brought a fundamental change in the position. The combination of England, Ireland and Scotland in a single monarchy gave a new unity to British politics, and meant that the government of the whole British Isles was bent, in the last resort, to serve the ends of a single interest. The immediate importance of this for Irish-Scottish relations was greatly increased by the fact that it coincided in time with the completion of the Tudor conquest of Ireland. A few days after Elizabeth's death Hugh O'Neill finally submitted to Mountjoy, the Nine Years' War was at an end, and the authority of the Dublin government was for the first time effective throughout Ireland. The destruction of Gaelic power in Ulster would, in any case, have tended to weaken the semi-independent chieftains of Western Scotland; but their position was more seriously threatened by the fact that the governments on both sides of the North Channel now served a common master and were directed to a common end. The power of the crown in both kingdoms was correspondingly strengthened. It could use Irish bases and Irish resources in its operations in the Western Isles, as in Sir John Campbell's expedition to Islay in 1614; and it could call in Scottish help to meet any new threat in Ulster, as when the Scottish council sent 200 troops during O'Doherty's short-lived rising in 1608.[1]

It must not be supposed that co-operation between the Scottish and Irish governments was close, continuous and effective. The character of seventeenth-century administration made such a development almost impossible. It was, for example, in the interest of both governments that cross-channel communications should be supervised.[2] But repeated attempts to enforce a passport system came to nothing: thieves, murderers, 'sturdy beggars', and (in the later part of the century) covenanting ministers, seem to have passed and repassed freely from one country to the other. It is true that the task of supervision was very difficult, for on both sides of the channel there were in-

numerable creeks and coves quite adequate for the small craft in
which the crossing was generally made. Yet it is difficult not to
believe that closer co-operation would have produced better
results. In spite of this sort of failure, however, the possibility
of joint action in times of crisis remained a factor of great importance throughout the century, witness the Scottish intervention
in Ulster in the 1640s and the readiness of the Irish government
to intervene in Scotland in the 1670s.

Probably the most significant result of the union of the crowns
for the future of Irish-Scottish relations was the establishment
of a new Scottish settlement in Ulster. There had long been in
north Antrim a settlement of MacDonnells, who, being Gaelic
and Roman Catholic, had mingled fairly easily with the native
population. But the newcomers of the early seventeenth century
were protestant lowlanders, and they brought a fresh element
into the life of the province. The way was opened by Hugh
Montgomery, laird of Braidstane, who had contacts with Ireland
through his brother, Thomas, a ship-master trading between
Scotland and Carrickfergus. Through this brother Montgomery struck a bargain with Con O'Neill of Clandeboye, an
unfortunate and somewhat shiftless landlord, who held some
60,000 acres in north Down. O'Neill was in trouble with the
government and Montgomery, who had some influence with
King James, offered to secure his pardon in return for half his
estate. The bargain was completed in form—that is, O'Neill got
his pardon, and a grant of half his estate was made out in favour
of Montgomery; but before the latter could take possession
another ambitious Scot, James Hamilton, whose influence with
the king was apparently greater than Montgomery's, induced
James to make an entirely new settlement, by which the whole
of the Clandeboye estate was divided, more or less equally, between O'Neill, Montgomery and Hamilton himself. Con O'Neill
proved no match for his new neighbours, and within a few years
they had got possession of almost all that the royal settlement
had left him.[3] But if Montgomery and Hamilton were not always
scrupulous in their methods, they were able and energetic
colonizers. Their estates, which were waste and depopulated
when they took possession of them, soon flourished. They
brought in stock, they planted settlers, they built houses, they
founded or re-founded towns. The prosperity of north Down, as

well as its strongly Scottish character, has its origin in their labours.

These settlements in County Down, and other settlements undertaken about the same time in County Antrim, were the work of individual adventurers. But over most of the rest of Ulster a more grandiose scheme of colonization was being organized directly by the crown; and in this also the Scots played an important part. The opportunity for this project was provided by the secret flight of O'Neill and O'Donnell. After O'Neill's submission to the crown in 1603 they had received a free pardon; O'Neill had been confirmed in his earldom of Tyrone and O'Donnell had been created early of Tyrconnel; both had retained possession of their vast estates, covering between them the greater part of the province of Ulster. But dissatisfaction with their loss of independence, and uneasiness about the future, led them to take flight to the continent in September 1607. This was regarded by the government as clear evidence of treason; their lands were declared forfeit to the crown; and plans were quickly drawn up for planting them with protestant settlers. It was James's intention that his Scottish subjects should take part in this great work, and in March 1609 the Scottish council received instructions concerning the allocation of lands to suitable 'undertakers'. In the following year it was relieved of this responsibility, and the direction of the whole plantation, Scottish as well as English, was concentrated in London. But there is no indication that this change did anything to discourage Scottish settlers; and, especially in the early days of the plantation, a large proportion of the tenant-farmers, even on estates granted to English undertakers, seem to have been lowland Scots. So great was the attraction of Ireland, indeed, that Scottish landlords complained that holdings on their estates were being left vacant; and in 1636 the council issued a proclamation forbidding the passage to Ireland of any tenant or labourer without a certificate from his landlord or from a justice of peace.[4]

One natural result of the plantation was a great increase in cross-channel traffic. As early as 1612 there were complaints that shipmasters on the west coast were taking advantage of this to raise their charges; but attempts to restrain them proved, as might be expected, abortive, and the same complaint is made in 1627. Despite the increase in traffic the facilities for transport remained primitive. The most popular route was that from Port Patrick to Donaghadee; but Port Patrick had neither quay nor harbour, so that the crossing had to be made in small open boats that could be drawn up on the shore. In the 1630s an attempt was made to raise money by public subscription to build a proper landing-place; but the response was very slight, and Port Patrick had no quay until the eighteenth century. Donaghadee seems to have had a harbour of some sort as early as 1616; but since the largest ships mentioned in connection with it are only of ten tons burden, it must have been of very modest dimensions.[5]

We may assume that the increased traffic between Scotland and Ireland reflected an increase in trade; but it is impossible to assess its volume. Some, perhaps much, of it was certainly a smuggling trade. The Ulster plantation soon had an exportable surplus of agricultural produce, for which Scotland was the most convenient market. It was the policy of the Scottish government, however, to exclude such commodities, at least until the price of home produce had reached a certain level; and throughout the century repeated attempts were made to prevent the importation of 'victual' from Ireland. The very frequency with which new sets of regulations were issued bears witness to their ineffectiveness. Ulster farmers could under-sell the Scots even in their own home market; it was impossible to guard the whole coast; and no penalties could prevent shippers and merchants from engaging in what must have been a profitable trade. Though the maintenance of this illegal commerce is not the concern of the present essay, it must be borne in mind as an illustration of the close connection between Ulster and Scotland and of the impossibility of keeping it under governmental control.

This frequency and ease of intercourse meant that the Scottish settlement in Ulster was not so much a separate colony as an extension of Scotland itself. It is significant that when the Scottish council was considering a fresh scheme for the control of cross-channel traffic, in 1624, it negotiated, not with the Irish government in Dublin, but directly with the leading Scottish landlords in north-east Ulster. Quite apart, however, from any such administrative action, Scots on both sides of the channel had common interests, and might, should occasion require it, unite in a common purpose. It was during the sharpening religious controversy of the 1630s that this community of interest first found significant expression.

One main purpose of the Ulster plantation was to strengthen the protestant population, and for this purpose Scottish protestants were as acceptable as English. To begin with, settlers from Scotland had no trouble with the established church in Ireland, despite the ecclesiastical differences between the two countries. The tone of the Irish church was at this time strongly puritanical, indeed Calvinistic; the Ulster bishops, some of whom were themselves Scots, made no attempt to enforce the act of uniformity strictly; and Scottish ministers were allowed to hold benefices with scant regard for the book of common prayer. So secure did they feel that they even took the offensive; Robert Blair, of Bangor, when called upon by the bishop to preach at the triennial visitation of 1626 delivered a sermon on the unscriptural character of episcopacy.[6] The extension of Laudian influence to Ireland under Wentworth's government put an end to this easy toleration, and in 1636 five of the more determined nonconformists among the Scottish ministers were deprived of their livings. Most of them retired to Scotland, whither they were later followed by others of similar views; and their influence helped to strengthen the opposition that Laud's policy was arousing there also. When this opposition took form in the National Covenant of 1638 the solidarity of Scots on both sides of the channel was clearly shown; not only was the covenant signed by Ulster Scots in Scotland at the time, but copies were soon being circulated for signature in Ulster also. Neither in Scotland itself, nor among the Scots in Ulster, did the covenant gain unanimous support, but it did provide the basis for an ecclesiastical alliance between the two areas; and it was this alliance that gave special significance to Irish-Scottish relations during the remainder of the seventeenth century.

The complicated train of events between 1638 and 1660 cannot here be followed in detail. The Irish insurrection of 1641, beginning among the native Irish of Ulster, helped to precipitate the civil conflict towards which England was already moving; and the whole of the British Isles was soon plunged into the 'War of the Three Kingdoms', which lasted with brief intermissions until Cromwell imposed an uneasy peace in 1651—a peace that proved to be a prelude to the restoration of the monarchy in 1660. For

our purpose, it is enough to note that these years saw the con-
solidation of the Ulster Scots as a community distinct both from
the native Irish and from the English settlers, and saw also the
strengthening of their links with Scotland.

The very dangers that threatened them contributed to these
ends. The outbreak of insurrection in October 1641, drove
hundreds of refugees across the channel, where they spread their
tales of terror and aroused the sympathetic anger of their com-
patriots. Public subscriptions were raised for their relief, and
preparations set on foot, by agreement with the English parliament, for sending 10,000 Scottish troops to Ulster. Delays in the
negotiations with parliament held things up, and it was not until
3rd April 1642 that the first contingent, 2,500 strong, landed at
Carrickfergus, under Major-General Robert Munro. By the
following August, when Alexander Leslie, earl of Leven, took
over the command, the full complement of 10,000 men had
arrived, and the effective strength of the army was further increased by the co-operation of forces raised locally among the
Ulster Scots. Though its operations were confined to Ulster,
and though it suffered a crushing defeat by Owen Roe O'Neill at
Benburb in June 1646, this army played an important part in the
Irish wars throughout the 1640s, and its presence gave the
Scottish community in the north a political importance that it
could not otherwise have had.

It was hardly less important that the arrival of a Scottish army
crystallized the ecclesiastical position. The ministers who accompanied Munro's advance force as chaplains set up sessions in
four of the regiments, and then constituted a presbytery, which
held its first meeting on 10th June 1642, at Carrickfergus.[7] The
example proved infectious. There was an immediate and widespread demand among the Scottish settlers, even from some who
had formerly supported Wentworth, for a general establishment
of the presbyterian system; and in July a petition claiming to
represent the wishes of 'the most part of the Scottish nation in
the north of Ireland' was addressed to the general assembly at St.
Andrews, asking that more ministers might be sent over. Presbyterianism thus emerged as the distinctive characteristic of the
Ulster Scots. When the restoration of the monarchy brought with
it the restoration of authority to the Church of Ireland they were
no longer, as in the early years of the century, a somewhat uneasy

group within the establishment, but an effectively-organized rival church, with which no compromise was possible. In the conditions of the time this was bound to be of more than merely ecclesiastical significance; and throughout the restoration period the attitude of the Ulster presbyterians was a source of anxiety not only to the Irish government but to the Scottish government as well.

The reimposition of episcopacy on the Church of Scotland in the 1660s kept much of the country in a state of almost constant disturbance. The bitterest opposition came from those who refused to be satisfied with toleration (or 'indulgence'), and demanded the full execution of the covenant. The fact that the main centre of the militant covenanters was in the south-west meant that the Scottish government could not ignore the danger presented by presbyterian Ulster, both as a source of supply and as a haven of refuge for actual and potential rebels. The Irish government, already uneasy about the state of the north, was equally alarmed at the possible influence of Scottish example; for though the Ulster presbyterians had much less to complain of than their co-religionists in Scotland, they were by no means reconciled to the ecclesiastical settlement of the restoration. The English government was hardly less concerned than those of Scotland and Ireland; for though the presbyterian party in England was politically weak, there was a hard core of disgruntled republicans (independents and anabaptists for the most part) who engaged in almost ceaseless plotting against the restored monarchy. At first sight, these men (Ludlow, Desborough, Roger Jones and their like) might seem to have little in common with those who supported the covenant. But conspiracy makes strange bedfellows, and their common hatred of episcopacy was a basis of co-operation more than sufficient to excite the alarm of the English government.

Col. Thomas Blood's plot in Ireland in 1663 indicated the kind of combination to be feared. The leaders were Cromwellian soldiers, but they had some support also among the presbyterians and tried to enlist more by combining with their promise of religious toleration a promise to accept the Solemn League and Covenant. Though the first step planned by the conspirators was the seizure of Dublin Castle, there can be little doubt that if it had succeeded it would have been the signal for risings not only

C

in Ulster but in England and Scotland as well. Throughout the restoration period the fear of such concerted action against the monarchy was kept alive by reports to government and by popular rumours. No doubt many of these reports were exaggerated, and some were invented—in the general atmosphere of suspicion that existed the trade of informer was a ready refuge for the unscrupulous. But the frequency with which we find these reports and rumours associating the presbyterians of Scotland and Ireland with the 'fanatics' of England suggests that there was a genuine fear of such a combination. The news of the Pentland rising of 1666 was followed at once by precautionary measures throughout the north of England, the mayor of York even going so far as to impose a ten o'clock curfew on the citizens. This fear was particularly strong in the early part of the period; but as late as 1683 Ormond was persuaded that the Rye House plot must have an Irish side to it, 'considering how many dissenters were in a body in the north . . . and the correspondence held betwixt that sort of people in the three kingdoms'.

This sense of common danger might have been expected to produce some co-ordination of policy between the three governments; but in fact such co-ordination was often lacking, and its absence sometimes extended the risk of disturbance. Any increase of severity in the treatment of the presbyterians in either Scotland or Ireland usually had its first effect on the more extreme among their leaders, and especially the ministers; when they found themselves in danger in one country they took refuge in the other, and continued their work there. Thus, at the very beginning of the restoration period the threat to the Ulster presbyterians led several of their ministers to move over to Scotland, and this probably accounts for an act passed by the Scottish parliament in February 1661, forbidding 'persons of all sorts' to come from Ireland without passes, a measure which Wodrow interpreted as being intended to 'prevent the retiring of the Scots presbyterians in the north of Ireland to their native country, now when they are beginning to feel the fury of the prelates there'.[8] The ineffectiveness of the restriction is shown by the fact that in the following September the council was trying to secure the arrest of Irish ministers who, despite the act, had arrived in Clydesdale. Again, in 1663, we find Ormond proposing a policy that would certainly have increased the exodus to Scotland. At the time of Blood's plot he had arrested as many as he could lay hands on of 'the Scottish silenced ministers in the north', though without quite knowing what to do with them. After some delay, he decided to release those who were willing to give bonds to leave the kingdom and not return without permission; and this, of course, meant that they would go to Scotland, as Ormond himself seems to have realized. At this point the English government intervened, and though Ormond defended his policy on the double grounds that the ministers would be more dangerous in Ireland than elsewhere, and that most of them really belonged to Scotland anyhow, he allowed them to remain.[9]

Despite Ormond's change of plan a good many Ulster ministers did in fact move over to Scotland about this time, and all precautionary measures on the Scottish side failed to check them. It was not, of course, a one-way traffic; and the Irish government was no more successful than the Scottish in controlling it. The most closely hunted of the covenanters—Michael Bruce, John Crookshank, Alexander Peden, Walsh, David Houston—landed in Ireland, moved about the country, and held conventicles, with remarkably little interference from the government. Even at times of crisis, as, for example, during the Pentland rising, when the Irish government was particularly alert to the danger of infection from Scotland, its efforts accomplished very little.

The Pentland crisis was too brief to produce any scheme of combined military operations, such as was to emerge during the more prolonged crisis of the 1670s; but before that second crisis arose there was a period of relaxation. In Scotland, this can be connected with the beginning of Lauderdale's supremacy. As early as September 1667, we find Archbishop Burnet of Glasgow complaining of a change: 'We are now (it seems) resolved to overcome our rebels with patience and lenity'.[10] This referred to a proclamation of indemnity, which was then under consideration in the Scottish council, and which was issued in the following month. As Lauderdale's control of Scottish affairs became more complete, he moved from indemnity to toleration. The first 'letter of indulgence' was issued in June 1669, and drew from Archbishop Burnet such a protest as caused him to be temporarily deprived of his see.[11]

Lauderdale's action may be regarded as part of the general

policy of toleration towards which Charles II was at this time moving; but it reflected also his own belief that the presbyterians could be conciliated by kindness. He was, perhaps, guided by expediency rather than by principle, and his aim was not so much to heal the divisions in the church as to strengthen the power of the monarchy. He realized how important for Scotland the attitude of the Ulster presbyterians was bound to be, and he kept himself informed of their affairs, mainly through his correspondence with Sir Arthur Forbes, marshal of the army in Ireland and afterwards earl of Granard. Forbes was of Scottish extraction and, although himself a conformist, was always ready to defend the political loyalty of the Ulster presbyterians. The more lenient treatment that they received during these years owes something to the combined influence of Forbes and Lauderdale; and these two were the main agents in securing the first grant of the *regium donum* in 1672.[12] This was an annual payment of £600 to the presbyterian ministers of Ulster; and, though it probably was not paid very regularly, it served the twofold purpose of placing the ministers under an obligation to the crown and of making them less completely dependent on their people.

This conciliation of the Ulster presbyterians was particularly important in view of what was happening in Scotland. The policy of indulgence, even though accompanied by Archbishop Leighton's scheme of conference and peaceful persuasion, could not satisfy the westland whigs. They stood out for a rigid adherence to the covenant, neglected the 'indulged' ministers, and continued to resort to field conventicles. Lauderdale's zeal for moderation was, as he explained to Leighton, cooled by such 'mad pranks, so evidently threatening a rebellion', and he now advocated a 'vigorous quelling of this spirit'. He took the view that those who refused to be satisfied by the indulgence deserved no consideration; and the attempt to suppress the whigs by military severity was resumed.

One of the first effects of this change of policy was an exodus of extremists to Ulster. But they met with a rather dubious welcome. There were some, of course, who received them as 'suffering saints'; but the settled presbyterian ministers of the province were content with the liberty they enjoyed of going unobtrusively about their work, and felt uneasy at the more public activity of covenanting preachers who stirred up the people by fiery sermons at great field conventicles. The covenanters, for their part, denounced the peaceable ministers for their tame submission to a prelatic government. Peden condemned Ireland (meaning the presbyterians of the country) for 'security and formality'; and James Renwick upbraided the Irish ministers 'to their face, for their defections, indifferency and lukewarmness in the cause of Christ'.[13]

Essex, at this time lord lieutenant of Ireland, was shrewd enough to see that these divisions, and the absence of any noted leader, made the Ulster presbyterians politically harmless, unless they should be goaded by severity into violent courses. So he followed a cautious policy; and even where the activities of the covenanting preachers led to open defiance of the law he refused to take strong measures. In the autumn of 1672 he compelled Bishop Mossom of Derry to compromise with the presbyterian leaders there; over a year later he prevented Sir George Rawdon from taking action against an offending presbyterian minister, who had been holding great meetings of presbyterians in the Lisburn area; and in 1674 we find him commending Bishop Hackett of Down for his moderation towards the dissenters. It is significant that in the summer of 1674 many of the refugee ministers left the comparative safety of Ireland to return home; they must have felt that if a blow were to be struck for the covenant it would be in Scotland and not in Ulster.

At this time it certainly seemed that Scotland was on the brink of a new insurrection, more extensive and more dangerous than that of 1666. The actual outbreak was, in fact, delayed for five years; but the interval was one of prolonged crisis, rendered more acute by the fear that a successful rising in Scotland would threaten the position of the monarchy throughout the British Isles. In these circumstances, Charles called on the Irish government for military help in meeting the danger. It was a very natural move: Ireland had a considerable standing army; an Irish force could be quickly transported to the main centre of disaffection, in Galloway; the Irish government had an immediate interest in suppressing any revolutionary move among presbyterians. Accordingly, in August 1674, Essex received formal instructions to send 2,000 foot and six troops of horse to the north of Ireland, to be ready for service in Scotland if required; and by October this 'northern brigade', as it was generally called, was established near Carrickfergus.[14] It remained there for a year, during which the situation in Scotland, though fairly quiet, showed no fundamental change. In September 1675 the 'brigade' was broken up; partly, perhaps, because the government's sense of urgency was less acute than it had been a year earlier, but mainly because of the practical difficulties in the way of maintaining so large a force in the same area for another winter.

The expedient of using Irish troops in this way, once hit upon, was soon repeated. In the summer of 1676, when the news from Scotland was more alarming, Essex was again instructed to concentrate forces in Ulster, and the 'northern brigade' was reconstituted and quartered for some months on the shores of Belfast Lough. A year later, in September 1677, Lauderdale asked the king to have a similar force sent there again, and instructions to this effect were at once despatched to Ormond, who had now succeeded Essex as lord lieutenant. Ormond took his task very seriously. Instead of sending so many troops and companies to the north *en bloc*, as Essex had done, he selected a fixed number of 'commanded men' from each troop and company of the army, and was thus able to build up a force of the men best fit for active service. The command of the brigade was entrusted, as before, to Lord Granard, who seems to have shared Ormond's determination to do the job thoroughly. 'It concerns me nearly', he wrote to Lord Conway, 'having good men to be able to give the best account of them I can'.[15] To this end, he made every possible preparation for an expedition to Scotland—he laid in a store of biscuit and other provisions, he prepared field-pieces, spades, picks and shovels, and he stopped all outward-bound shipping until further order, so as to make sure of transport for his force. This time the 'brigade' remained in being from 1st November 1677, when it held its rendezvous at Lambeg racecourse, near Belfast, until March 1678. It was broken up, partly because of the heavy expense, and partly because the Scottish government's latest method of dealing with the covenanters seemed to have been, at least for the time being, successful.

This new method was the occupation of the disaffected shires by a large body of highland troops—the 'Highland Host'—who would be strong enough to overawe the local inhabitants. This course was decided on in December 1677, and put into operation early in the following year. By 1st February Lauderdale could

tell Granard that there were at least 7,000 foot and 1,000 horse
in the shires of Ayr, Renfrew and Lanark; and, he added, 'this
force will, I hope, do the business'. It was said that Lauderdale
hoped that the 'Highland Host' would goad the covenanters into
open rebellion, so that he could crush them once for all. If so,
this may have been the meaning behind his comment to Granard.
More probably, however, all he meant was that he now had
enough troops to keep order without relying on help from Ireland; and this is borne out by the fact that not long afterwards it
was decided in London, presumably on advice from Scotland,
that the 'northern brigade' should be recalled.

The depredations of the 'Highland Host' neither provoked an
insurrection nor produced a lasting peace. The western shires
were temporarily cowed; but when the highlanders had been
withdrawn the covenanters resumed their activity. It is possible
that they were encouraged by the growing strength of the opposition to Lauderdale, an opposition led by the duke of Hamilton,
and supported not only by a group of Scottish nobles but by a
considerable faction in the English parliament. For the time
being, however, Lauderdale retained the king's confidence, and
continued his policy of repression in spite of all criticism. It was
as a result of this repression rather than of any formed design
that open insurrection broke out at the end of May 1679. A few
weeks later, the insurgents were decisively defeated at Bothwell
Brig by a combined English and Scottish force under the duke of
Monmouth. Three times during the previous five years the king
had ordered Irish forces to be prepared for a descent upon Scotland if rebellion should break out there; now, when rebellion
actually occurred, it was from England, and not from Ireland,
that military help was drawn. The reasons for the change were,
at least in part, political. Monmouth, who was given command of
the expedition, was, by his marriage with the heiress of Buccleuch,
a Scottish duke, and it was hoped that this would make him
acceptable in Scotland. Besides this, the 'popish plot' scare was
now in full swing; and, though the Irish army was in fact composed exclusively of protestants, its use in any part of Great
Britain would almost certainly have been denounced as the bringing in of papists to put down the protestant religion. Towards the
middle of June, when news from Scotland was still very bad,
Ormond was in fact instructed, in rather vague terms, to prepare

some military aid for the Scottish government, and by that time he had already, on his own initiative, concentrated some forces in Ulster; but the insurrection was crushed so quickly that Ormond had little more to do than look out for refugees.

From 1679 until the downfall of James VII and II this remained the principal duty of the Irish government in relation to Scottish affairs. In 1685, indeed, there was some talk of sending Irish troops to assist in suppressing Argyll's rebellion; but that unhappy enterprise was so ill-managed that it collapsed almost of itself. When, three years later, the long-considered project of using Irish troops in Great Britain was at last carried out, they were brought not to Scotland but to England, and with disastrous results for the monarchy.

This brief survey of the military preparations in Ireland raises three questions. What system of communication was maintained between the governments in Edinburgh and Dublin? What was the position of the Ulster presbyterians? Did Ireland, in fact, contribute anything to the suppression of the westland whigs?

From the very beginning of the restoration period it was recognized that if the Scottish and Irish governments were to keep in touch with one another there must be some regular postal service between the two countries. In September 1662 the Scottish council established a horse post between Edinburgh and Port Patrick, and a packet-boat service from thence to Donaghadee; and in December it was agreed that there should be a regular weekly post, by this route, between Edinburgh and Dublin.[16] It is not clear how well this system worked; but it cannot have lasted very long, for in 1667 the king had to recommend to the Scottish council the establishment of a postal service with Ireland, pointing out that it was necessary to the royal service that a 'way of correspondence' should be regularly maintained between the governments of the two kingdoms. The council appointed a committee to examine the question, but nothing seems to have been done at this time.

The maintenance of regular communications became more urgent in 1674, with the prospect of an Irish force being sent to Scotland. But throughout Essex's time correspondence between the governments seems to have been a matter of *ad hoc* arrangement; and for early news of what was happening in Scotland Essex had to depend mainly on reports forwarded to him by Sir

George Rawdon, who lived at Lisburn in County Antrim and managed the Irish estates of his brother-in-law, Lord Conway. When Ormond returned to the lord lieutenancy in 1677 things improved somewhat. The Scottish council re-established the horse-post between Edinburgh and Port Patrick, and a new packet-boat service with Donaghadee was started, operated this time from the Irish side. Sir George Rawdon, who managed this part of the business, was unfortunate in his choice of an agent, who turned out to be a sympathizer with the disaffected party in Scotland, and kept the conspirators informed of what was going on. But, despite these arrangements, we find Ormond complaining to Coventry, in June 1678: 'There is a post, but no correspondence settled betwixt this place [Dublin] and Edinburgh, at least not betwixt the government there and here'.[17] Later on, however, he succeeded in establishing closer relations with the Scottish government, which were maintained until his recall in 1685.

The maintenance of an effective postal service was not the only difficulty in the way of satisfactory relations between the Irish and Scottish governments. There was a constitutional difficulty also. The governments of Ireland and Scotland were both, though in different ways, subject to direction from England. The English council, or one of its committees, maintained regular supervision over Irish affairs, and even comparatively minor matters were commonly referred to England for decision. Scotland was, in theory, completely free of English control and dependent solely on the king. But though the king did not make use of English constitutional machinery in dealing with Scottish affairs, as he did in dealing with Irish affairs, yet in practice the government at Edinburgh was hardly more at liberty to act on its own initiative than was the government at Dublin. The result was that Irish-Scottish co-operation depended upon direction from England, and could go no further than such direction warranted. It is significant that most of the efforts to establish, or maintain, a postal service between the two countries were undertaken at the instigation of the king or his English advisers; and even when the suggestion originated in Scotland or Ireland it was passed on, in the first place, to the authorities in London.

The effect of this constitutional position appears clearly in a proposal put forward by Essex in September 1674, when it seemed likely that he might have to send military help to Scotland:

> In regard that intelligence may be long in coming from London hither, and that the notice of any troubles, if such should happen in Scotland, must first be sent from thence to London and then orders transmitted hither I do humbly offer to his majesty's consideration, whether it may not be convenient an order be sent hither directing me that upon certain intelligence of any commotions in Scotland (for I have appointed Sir Arthur Forbes to send over two or three men, and maintain them there on purpose to give us true and early accounts of affairs) I should forthwith appoint these men to embark: as also that a commission may be ready on the other side to meet Sir Arthur Forbes upon his landing there.[18]

There is no indication that Essex received the order he asked for, and in any case the danger that the Irish force had been prepared to meet did not arise. But in 1677, when a similar force was assembled on the Ulster coast, the same question was raised again, not only by Granard, who commanded the 'northern brigade', but by Lauderdale also. In November he wrote to Danby:

> Now my humble desire is that the king would send immediate orders into Ireland, that my Lord Granard may come over into Scotland upon the first call from the king's privy council in Scotland . . . You may assure his majesty we shall not call for that party out of Ireland if we find we can probably do his business without them, but if what we propose here in this kingdom should not answer our expectation, it will be too late to send for orders, and therefore I hope the king will trust us here to send such order to Ireland.[19]

Lauderdale's proposal was at once accepted, and orders to this effect were sent to Ormond. The forces prepared at the same time in the north of England were similarly placed at the disposal of the Scottish council. The necessity for making such special arrangements as those of 1674 and 1677 shows very clearly that however willing the Scottish and Irish government might be to co-operate in face of a common danger they could not carry that co-operation very far without explicit authority from England. At the decision-making level, Irish-Scottish relations appear simply as a branch of English policy.

It would be misleading, however, to consider the Irish government as being, at least in this matter, a mere tool of the English council. It had a direct interest of its own in the suppression of the westland whigs, whose activities were potentially a danger to the peace of Ulster. Opinions about the extent of this danger varied. In the summer of 1676, at the very time when he was preparing troops for service in Scotland, Essex was less alarmed about affairs there than about reports that the covenant was being taken in County Londonderry. This alarm continued into the following year, when covenanting preachers were not only active in Ulster but had penetrated into northern Connaught.[20] Reports from Archbishop Boyle and Sir George Rawdon show that these preachers had a popular following, and express fears of what might happen in Ulster if there were any upheaval in Scotland. Ormond apparently shared these fears. When he heard of the defeat of the covenanters at Bothwell Brig he wrote to Sir Robert Southwell, 'It was time to send us good news out of Scotland; the brethren in all parts of this kingdom, especially in the north, were growing very bold, and ready to come in to bear a part, if those of Scotland had had success'.[21] And a few weeks later he wrote to Lord Burlington, 'I was not without some apprehensions of the common sort of Scots in the north, being well assured that their false teachers held correspondence with their brethren in Scotland'. But when he was charged with slandering the loyalty of Irish protestants in general Ormond modified his expressions considerably, and confined his accusations to 'some very few inconsiderable persons of the non-conformists'.

Against these varied expressions of distrust may be set the opinion of Lord Granard, who probably knew the Ulster presbyterians better than any other important official of government and who was convinced that the bulk of them were loyal to the crown. In March 1678 he sent Ormond a declaration of loyalty signed by the leading presbyterian ministers in Ulster. In 1679 copies of this, or of a similar declaration, were being circulated; and in the summer of 1680 four Ulster ministers, at the instigation of Sir Hans Hamilton, of County Armagh, signed a letter against taking up arms against the crown, and this was presented to the king by Lord Granard. These declarations certainly reflected the opinion of the bulk of the settled presbyterian ministers of Ulster, but they were naturally distasteful to the covenanters. Patrick Walker's garbled account of the signing of the declarations illustrates the attitude of the refugees from Scotland towards the tamer policy of the Ulster Scots, and is also, incidentally, a fair example of the kind of story that won for Alexander Peden the title of 'prophet':

> In that short time he was in Ireland, the government required all presbyterian ministers in Ireland, that they should give it under their hand, that they had no accession to the late rebellion at Bothwell Bridge in Scotland, and that they did not approve of it; which the most part did, and sent Mr. Thomas Gowans, a Scotsman, and one Mr. Paton from the north of Ireland, to Dublin, to present it to the lord lieutenant; the which when Mr. Peden heard, he said, Mr. Gowans and his brother Paton are sent and gone the devil's errand, but God shall arrest them by the gate; accordingly, Mr. Gowans by the way was struck by a sore sickness, and Mr. Paton fell from his horse and broke or crushed his leg.

Their quiescence was a tribute to the success of the moderate policy followed by the Irish government; and this moderation, though in one way it may have complicated things for the Scottish council by leaving Ulster as a haven of refuge for persecuted covenanters, was probably on balance a contribution to the peace of Scotland. It is not unreasonable to suppose that had there been another Galloway in the north-east of Ireland the likelihood of an explosion would have been greatly increased.

Any attempt to assess the value of the military preparations of the Irish government must be equally speculative, for no Irish troops were in fact sent to Scotland. It is hardly likely, however, that the 'northern brigade' of 1674–5 would have been reconstituted in 1676 and again in 1677 unless its presence in Ulster had had a good effect in Scotland. Lauderdale's opinion, in December 1677, was 'it hath been of great use to the king's service that the party is so near, and hath damped the disaffected, and I beg they may continue on that coast'. It is perhaps not without significance that the covenanters began their insurrection at a time when there was no Irish force ready to move across the channel at a moment's notice.

The union of the three kingdoms in 1603 had marked a change in the character of Irish-Scottish relations; so did the revolution of 1688–90. In the post-revolution era social and economic links between the two countries continued, and in some respects grew stronger; but Irish-Scottish relations ceased to have the urgent political significance that had formerly attached to them. No doubt various partial and subsidiary explanations of this change can be put forward, but the fundamental reason lies in the ecclesiastical position. The Ulster presbyterians, though profoundly dissatisfied with their treatment, were convinced that they must stand by the revolution settlement. The Scottish danger now came not from the remnant of covenanters but from the Jacobite highlanders, whom no party in Ireland was willing, or, if willing, able, to help. The events of 1715–16 showed the true character of the situation. The Irish Roman Catholics, though strong in numbers and Jacobite in sympathy, were too cowed to act; the Ulster presbyterians defied the sacramental test, imposed on them in 1704, and flocked into the militia to defend the protestant succession. In this essential point the Scots of Ireland were at one both with their brethren in Scotland and with the ruling class in Ireland—they had ceased to represent an independent political interest.

NOTES

1. By a curious coincidence, it had been arranged, shortly before O'Doherty's insurrection broke out, to send some hundreds of troops from Ireland to Scotland. (Privy Council to Chichester, 26th Apr. 1608 (*Cal. S.P., Ire.*, 1606–8, p. 487).)
2. Chichester to Privy Council, 11th Apr. 1608 (ibid., p. 470); *Register of the Privy Council of Scotland* (3rd series), i. 439–42.
3. D. A. Chart, 'Break-up of the estate of Con O'Neill', in *Proceedings of the Royal Irish Academy*, xlviii, C, pp. 119–44 (1942–3).
4. *Register of the Privy Council of Scotland* (2nd series), vi. 198.
5. J. Stevenson, *Two Centuries of Life in Down*, pp. 246–52.
6. J. S. Reid, *Presbyterian Church in Ireland* (ed. Killen), i. 132.
7. Reid, *Presbyterian Church in Ireland*, i. 372.
8. R. Wodrow, *Sufferings of the Church of Scotland* (ed. 1828–31), i. 108.
9. Ormond to Legge, 25th June 1663 (H.M.C. *Dartmouth*, i. 11); Ormond to Bennet, 25th June, 8th July, 15th Aug. 1663 (*Cal S.P. Ire.*, *1663–5*, pp. 149–50, 162, 201–2).
10. Abp. Burnet to Abp. Sheldon, 23rd Sept. 1667 (*Lauderdale Papers*, ii. appendix, p. 6).
11. P. Hume Brown, *History of Scotland*, ii. 401–2.

12. *Presbyterian Loyalty* (Belfast, 1713), pp. 383–5; R. Hamilton to Lauderdale, 5th Nov. [1672] (*Lauderdale Papers*, ii. 229–30).

13. For the attitude of a contemporary Ulster presbyterian minister to covenanter preachers from Scotland see Patrick Adair, *True Narrative* (ed. Killen), pp. 257–61.

14. Forbes to Essex, 17th, 23rd Aug. 1674 (B. M. Stowe, 205, pp. 394, 409); same to same,—Oct. 1674 (B. M. Stowe, 206, pp. 127–8).

15. Granard to Conway, Belfast, 3rd Nov. 1677 (*Cal. S.P. Dom., 1677–8*, p. 440).

16. *Register of the Privy Council of Scotland* (3rd series), 1, 263; Samuel Bathurst to [Bennet], 10th Dec. 1662 (*Cal. S.P. Ire.*, 1660–2, p. 644).

17. Ormond to Coventry, 4th June 1678 (H.M.C. *Ormonde*, New Series, iv. 61, 66–7).

18. Essex to Danby, 12th Sept. 1674 (B. M. Stowe, 214, ff. 276–8).

19. Lauderdale to Danby, 8th Nov. 1677 (*Lauderdale Papers*, iii. 89–90).

20. Bp. Otway of Killala to Essex, 22nd Jan. 1676–7 (*Essex Papers*, ii. 94–5).

21. Ormond to Sir Robert Southwell, 23rd June 1679 (H.M.C. *Ormonde* Old Series, ii. 288).

Three

The Confederation of Kilkenny
Reviewed

MORE than a century has passed since the publication of the first
history of the Confederation of Kilkenny, by C. P. Meehan—a
slight sketch, based largely on Carte's *History of James, duke of
Ormond*, and intended to edify as well as inform the general
reader.[1] Since Meehan's time, a great body of documentary
material bearing on the period of the Confederation has appeared
in print. This is not the place for a detailed bibliographical survey, which would require a paper in itself; but reference must
be made to three collections of documents. Sir John Gilbert's
Contemporary history of affairs in Ireland and *History of the Irish
confederation and the war in Ireland* are, in name, editions of contemporary narratives; but the voluminous appendices, which
occupy the greater part of the space, contain so many letters and
papers from Irish, English, and continental sources that the two
collections might, by themselves, serve as a basis for a detailed
history of the Confederation.[2] A third contemporary narrative,
dealing with Rinuccini's nunciature in Ireland, has been edited
by Fr. Stanislaus Kavanagh and published by the Irish Manu-
scripts Commission.[3] It embodies a great mass of documents,
less varied in interest than those printed by Gilbert, but of
equal importance.

Though the first of these three collections appeared almost
eighty years ago, and though the period with which they are concerned is of great interest and obvious importance, the work of
interpretation has lagged far behind the publication of source
material. An enlarged edition of Meehan's book, incorporating
some of the material published by Gilbert, appeared in 1882. A
brief essay, entitled 'The Confederation of Kilkenny', contributed by James Donelan to R. B. O'Brien's *Studies in Irish*

47

History, 1603–1649 (Dublin, 1906), is not so much a study of the Confederation as a general survey of Irish history between 1641 and 1649. The same period is covered, in much greater detail, in the second volume of Richard Bagwell's *Ireland under the Stuarts* (London, 1909) and in Diarmid Coffey's *O'Neill and Ormond* (Dublin, 1914); neither of these, however, makes the history of the Confederation its central theme. More recently, some valuable specialized studies have appeared in learned periodicals;[4] but the need for a comprehensive history of the Confederation remains.[5]

This paper does not attempt even a summary survey of the whole Confederation period. Its purpose is to examine the Confederation, considered as an organization expressive of Irish national feeling; and it treats of political and military events only as they illustrate this theme.

'Confederation of Kilkenny' is a historian's term, of modern origin; the earliest use of it that I have been able to find is in the title of C. P. Meehan's book, published in 1846. The term thus came into currency at a time when its meaning had so altered as to be not only inapplicable but dangerously misleading. The Confederates themselves did not speak of their system as a 'confederation'. The title that they used officially was 'The Confederate Catholics of Ireland', and we find occasional less formal variations.[6] But even if they had used the word 'confederation' it would have borne a rather different meaning from that to which it had become restricted by the nineteenth century. By that time it meant, as it does today, a permanent, or semi-permanent, alliance of states, or at least of politically organized groups. In the seventeenth century it could also have meant an alliance of individuals, bound together in pursuit of a common purpose.[7] This is the sense behind one of the rare uses of the word in any Confederate document. Richard Bellings, in his defence of the policy of a cessation of arms (July 1643) writes as follows: 'By an oath of confederation we have bound ourselves to carry on the war for our faith, our king, and our country'.[8] The oath to which he here refers (most commonly known as the 'oath of association') was an oath taken by individuals, and was individually binding; neither in form nor in substance did it constitute an alliance or pact between separately organized groups or territories.[9]

This distinction is not merely a matter of verbal nicety. Both in composition and in organization the 'Confederate Catholics of Ireland' appeared to have some of the elements of a confederation, in the modern sense; and the use of the term 'Confederation of Kilkenny' tends to give these elements undue prominence, or at least to disguise the fact that they were incidental and not essential parts of the system. The most obvious and most important of these elements was the combination of the native Irish, with whom the insurrection of October 1641 originated, and the Old English, who joined with them before the end of that year.[10] At first sight, indeed, we seem to have here the basis of a genuine confederation. By December, when the union between the Ulster Irish and the recusant lords and gentry of the pale took place, the former had already established so much of a political system as was necessary for the raising and maintaining of their forces, and the palesmen had made use of the existing machinery of county organization to meet together and discuss the policy they were to follow.[11] The dramatic meeting on Crofty Hill, when Lord Gormanston formally demanded of Rory O'More and the Ulstermen wherefore they came armed into the pale, was not a casual encounter, but a carefully-staged demonstration, intended to give both parties an opportunity of declaring their principles in public. The union of which this meeting marks the formal beginning, and which was subsequently extended to include native Irish and Old English in almost every part of the kingdom, was not a harmonious one; for though both parties professed the same principles and subscribed the same oath of association, their political and economic interests were not identical. Friction, rivalry, and distrust between them continued throughout the whole period of the war, and contributed in some measure to their defeat. But this makes it all the more important to remember that the continued existence of distinct racial groups within the system of government that they had jointly set up was directly contrary to their professed intentions. The General Assembly, which was their parliament, and the Supreme Council, which was their executive, were elected on a territorial basis, and the very use of the terms 'native Irish' and 'old English' was condemned:[12]

And it is further ordered and established, that there shall be no distinction or comparison made betwixt old Irish, and old and

D

new English, or betwixt septs or families, or betwixt citizens and townsmen and countrymen, joining in union. . . .

This territorial basis, however, suggests another way in which the Confederates' organization had some element of a modern confederation. In the early stages of the war the provinces had tended to act as separate units. The ecclesiastical congregation which met at Kilkenny in May 1642, and which prepared the way for the first General Assembly, which met there in the following October, thought it necessary to decree that 'embassage sent from one province to foreign nations shall be held as made from the rest of the provinces', and that 'great men taken prisoner in one province may not be set at liberty . . . without the consent of the prelates and nobility of the other provinces united'.[13] When a regular system of government was instituted, the separate rights of the provinces were still recognized. The Supreme Council consisted of an equal number of members from each province, and though the final election was made by the General Assembly as a whole, it had to choose from lists drawn up by the members from each province, acting in separate groups.[14] Again, the military organization was provincial: there was a separate army and a separate commander for each province, and there was no commander-in-chief.[15] On these grounds, it might seem reasonable to describe the system of government as a confederation of the four provinces.[16]

The force of this argument, however, is outweighed by other considerations. The final authority in the Confederate system was the General Assembly, to which the Supreme Council was responsible. It was composed in the same way as parliament: that is to say, of spiritual and temporal lords, with representatives of the counties, and of those cities and boroughs normally represented in parliament.[17] Thus it had a direct relationship to the kingdom as a whole, and there was no deliberate balance of representation between the provinces. Secondly, though the Supreme Council was constituted on a provincial basis, its rules of procedure enabled decisions to be made without the assent, or even the presence, of members from all four provinces.[18] Thus the system of government established by the Confederates was, in purpose and effect, a unitary one: the first General Assembly explicitly laid down:[19]

that no temporal government or jurisdiction shall be assumed, kept, or exercised in this kingdom, or within any county or province thereof, during these troubles, other than is before expressed, by this General Assembly or the Supreme Council.

Finally, the maintenance in each province of a district army under its own commander was in part a matter of convenience in conducting a scattered war of sieges and skirmishes, and in part a reflection of problems of personal relationship: Thomas Preston and Owen Roe O'Neill were the leading Confederate generals, and neither would serve under the other. But though there was no commander-in-chief, the war was, as far as possible, directed from the centre; the Supreme Council appointed the provincial commanders and issued instructions to them.[20] In short, the fact that military organization was on a provincial basis gives no support to the view that the Confederate system of government was, in any formal way, a confederation of the four provinces.

The true nature of what we call the Confederation of Kilkenny appears most clearly when we consider the importance attached by the Confederates to the 'oath of association'. The first formal proposals for uniting the whole body of the insurgents throughout the kingdom under a single government seem to have been those put forward in the provincial synod held by Archbishop O'Reilly of Armagh, at Kells, on 22nd March 1641/2; and in these proposals an oath occupies a significant place:[21]

> Erigatur statim concilium ex personis simul ecclesiasticis et saecularibus sufficientibus: iuret nobilitas saecularis et clerus se observaturos debitam correspondentiam: coniuret in correctionem severam offensarum, exhibendo concilio et legibus et statutis factis et faciendis.

The congregation at Kilkenny in the following May expanded this proposal, and linked the necessity for an oath even more firmly with the necessity for securing obedience to the proposed governing council.[22] Finally, the first General Assembly decreed:[23]

> that to prevent the springing up of all national distinctions, the oath of association or union be taken solemnly, after confession and receiving the sacrament in the parish churches, throughout the kingdom, and the names of all the persons of rank and quality

in every parish that take the same to be enrolled in parchment, and to be returned, signed and sealed by the parish priest, to the ordinary of every diocese, who is to keep the same in his treasury. . . .

The taking of this oath was enforced by the threat of excommunication, and though it was considered particularly important that the nobility and gentry should conform, it was intended to be taken by persons of all ranks.[24]

The Confederation thus appears as an alliance of individuals, bound by oath to the pursuit of common objects, and in this respect it suggests a comparison with the Scottish national covenant of 1638.[25] But the position of the Scottish covenanters was different from that of the Irish Confederates; they had possession of the capital, and control of the machinery of government, so that, however revolutionary their actions might be in fact, they had the appearance of legality that comes from the use of wonted forms. The Irish Confederates, on the other hand, had to improvise a new government in open rivalry with the royal government already established in the capital; there had to be some basis on which the new government could claim allegiance; and that basis was the oath of association.

It was particularly significant that the oath of association was also an oath of allegiance to the crown. This was more than an empty assertion of loyalty, such as rebels have often used to disguise the true nature of their actions. In effect, it involved acceptance of a constitutional position against which almost the whole of Gaelic Ireland had been in revolt less than fifty years earlier; and it committed the Confederates to maintaining the English connexion, though they might dispute the terms on which it was to be settled. The loyalty of the Confederates was no doubt based on self-interest, and it was certainly not unconditional; but it was an important factor in the political situation, and it must be taken into account in any assessment of the Confederation as a 'national' movement.

This loyalty to the Crown was insisted upon from the first outbreak of the insurrection in Ulster in October 1641. The spurious royal commission exhibited by Sir Phelim O'Neill[26] probably brought him no support that he would not otherwise have had, and the insurgents soon dropped the claim to be acting under the direct authority of the king; but they never ceased to maintain that they were his loyal subjects, and that they were fighting in defence of his prerogative. Their first public declaration setting out their reasons for taking arms begins with the assertion that 'we, the Roman Catholics of this kingdom of Ireland, have been continual loving and faithful subjects to his sacred majesty';[27] and the 'gentry and commonalty' of County Cavan, in a remonstrance issued a few days later, declare that they 'harbour not the least thought of disloyalty towards his majesty, or purpose any hurt to any of his highness's subjects in their possession, goods or liberty'.[28] Indeed, one of the main grounds on which the insurgents justified their taking arms was the invasion of the royal prerogative by the 'puritan faction' in England and Scotland, which they not unreasonably regarded as a threat to their own religion.[29]

It was this declared loyalty of the northern insurgents that made possible a union with the lords and gentry of the pale. In a 'humble apology', drawn up after the union, the latter assure the king that they would rather 'sacrifice all our fortunes, estates, and lives in the defence of your crown and kingdom, than join with them [the Ulstermen] in drawing our swords contrary to our allegiance and duty against your sacred majesty, our dread and only sovereign lord'; but, they go on, the Ulster forces have given them 'full assurance' of their loyalty, and of the justice of their cause.[30]

Along with their professions of loyalty and of their determination to protect the royal prerogative, the insurgents put forward two more specific grounds for taking arms: the defence of the Roman Catholic church, and the redress of national grievances; thus we have from the beginning the triple programme tersely expressed in the motto of the Confederation *Pro Deo, pro rege, pro patria*.[31] The three elements in this programme were closely linked. In 1641 the Irish recusants enjoyed a considerable measure of practical toleration; but this, having no basis in law, depended on royal favour, and would certainly be swept away if the puritan party in the English parliament got control of affairs. Again, the main national grievances alleged in the insurgents' early declarations and remonstrances were the exclusion of Roman Catholics from opportunities for education and from public office, the maladministration of justice, and the confiscation of estates on flimsy excuses; there was little reason to suppose that an English puritan parliament would make any concessions on such matters. It was almost inevitable, therefore, that the Irish Roman Catholics should exalt the royal prerogative against puritan and parliamentary attack, and should place their hopes of re-settling the government of Ireland in a manner more satisfactory to themselves on an understanding with the king. Nor was it surprising that their first step towards reaching such an understanding should have been to take arms; this method had been employed by the Scots with a success which, at least in 1641, seemed to justify others in following their example. In their 'humble petition', drawn up in December 1641, 'the lords, knights, gentlemen, and others, inhabitants of the English pale of Ireland' defend their union with the Ulster insurgents, and beg that the king 'would make no worse construction of us for what we have done, than our loyalty and affection to your majesty do deserve, and no worse than your majesty hath made of others of your subjects, who upon less or the same occasions have done the like'.[32] And in the statement of the Confederates' case printed (in French) at Lille (January 1642/3) it is expressly stated that they were moved to take arms by the example of the Scots.[33]

The Confederates' readiness to defend the royal prerogative had a direct bearing on their view of the constitutional relationship between the two kingdoms; along with their exaltation of the king's authority went a denial that the English parliament had any right to legislate for Ireland. The Confederate lords of the pale, in urging the nobility and gentry of Galway to join with them (29th December 1641), express their purpose in taking up arms as being to 'vindicate the honour of our soverign, assure the liberty of our consciences, and preserve the freedom of this kingdom, under the sole obedience of his sacred majesty. . . .' In writing to Clanricard two months later (23rd February 1641/2), they make the last point more explicitly: they are fighting 'for the liberty of this our country, which the parliament of England (our fellow-subjects) seeketh to captivate and enthral to themselves. . . .' The same purpose is expressed in the 'Humble petition of the Catholics of Ireland', sent to Ormond to be forwarded to the king (31st July 1642) and signed by Gormanston and about thirty other lords and gentlemen. They have taken arms, they say, 'to that end only, that you, our gracious sovereign . . . might alone reign over us; and we, in the just freedom of subjects, independent of any jurisdiction, not derived from your majesty, live happily under the crown of England'.[34]

This insistence on parliamentary independence, which later gave rise to much debate during the negotiations for peace, was undoubtedly stimulated by the contemporary attitude of the English parliament towards Ireland, and especially by its passing of legislation for the confiscation of two and a half million acres of Irish land.[35] But it was not a new issue raised by the Confederates, who simply continued a campaign begun in the Irish house of commons in the spring of 1641.[36] The continuity is strongly marked. Many of the Confederates had, as members of the house of commons, taken part in the debates and negotiations connected with the claims then put forward; and Patrick Darcy, aftrewards the leading constitutional lawyer of the Confederation, had been chosen by the commons as their prolocutor in a conference with the house of lords, to present the case for the legislative independence of the Irish parliament.[37] It is significant that the 'Argument' which he then delivered was first printed at Waterford, in 1643, by Thomas Bourke, 'printer to the Confederate Catholics of Ireland'.[38] The date of publication is important, for it was this year that saw the beginning of formal negotiations between Ormond and the Confederates, which led first to a cessation of arms (September 1643) and then to the peace of 1646. In all these negotiations one of the points most strongly insisted on by the Confederate commissioners was that the independence of the Irish parliament should be asserted.[39]

The strong interest taken by the Confederates in the constituional claims of the Irish parliament has a special significance when considered in the light of the dual character of the Confederate movement. On the one hand, the Confederates could claim, with some show of reason, to be, in fact, the Irish nation, and such a claim might be said to be implicit in their conduct of affairs; they lived under a government devised by themselves, they raised and directed their own armies and their own fleet, they maintained diplomatic relations with the powers of Europe. On the other hand, the Confederate movement was a party organization, a 'confederation' (in the seventeenth-century sense) of a section of the population associated for the attainment of particular objects; the Confederates were, to use the terms in which they described themselves in their dealings with Ormond, 'his majesty's Roman Catholic subjects . . . now in arms'.[40]

In retrospect, it is natural that the former character should appear the more striking, and some historians have represented the Confederation of Kilkenny as primarily an expression of Irish nationalism and the General Assembly as the true parliament of the kingdom.[41] But to the Confederates themselves one of the most important factors in the situation was that the Assembly was *not* a true parliament; it was a temporary expedient: 'they were necessitated', they explained to Ormond, 'to rule and govern their party to avoid the extirpation of their religion and nation, plotted and contrived by the said malignant party, and to preserve his majesty's rights, and their proceedings were and are as near and consonant to the laws of the kingdom as the state and condition of the times did or can permit'.[42] Their object was not to perpetuate their new government, but to obtain a settlement of their claims in a legal parliament.[43] It was because they wanted this settlement to be secure from interference by the English parliament that they insisted on the independence of the Irish parliament being recognized.

In so far, then, as the Confederate movement was a 'national' one, it represented a continuing development within the existing constitutional framework; it looked backward to Magna Carta, rather than to any tradition of Gaelic independence,[44] and it based its claims on legal precedent, not on general principles: 'this your majesty's kingdom of Ireland in all successions of ages since the reign of King Henry II . . . had parliaments of their own, composed of lords and commons, qualified with equal liberties, powers, privileges and immunities with the parliament of England, and only dependent of the crown of England and Ireland'.[45] This may be bad history and doubtful law; but it is a fair indication of the attitude of the men who wrote it towards the character and rights of the Irish nation.

The validity of this description of the character of the Confederate movement must be tested by reference to the internal disputes which divided the Confederates; for though these disputes arose (at least ostensibly) out of questions of ecclesiastical policy, they involved other factors, bearing on the general character of the Confederation and its place in the tradition of Irish nationalism. In their negotiations with Ormond for a settlement of religion the Confederates found themselves in a dilemma. By their oath of association, by their professions to foreign powers, and by their own actions within the territories they controlled, they were committed to a policy of establishing the Roman Catholic church on a basis of legal security. But how was this to be reconciled with the policy, to which they were also committed, of supporting the royal prerogative and the existing law of the land?

There was an obvious theoretical solution to this dilemma in the claim that the anti-papal legislation was invalid. Such a claim is perhaps implied in the 'Humble petition of the Catholics of Ireland', addressed to the king in December 1642, in which they express their determination 'to observe and to be ruled only by your common laws of England, and statutes here established and enacted by parliament among us, which are not contrary to our Catholic Roman religion . . .';[46] and in the third of the four 'propositions' added to the oath of association in January 1646/7 it is required that all laws and statutes made since the twentieth year of King Henry VIII whereby any restraint was laid on clergy or laity in the exercise of the Roman Catholic religion or of 'their several functions, jurisdictions, and privileges' should be 'repealed, revoked, and declared void' by act of parliament.[47] But the very demand for an act of repeal shows the weakness of the legal ground on which the Confederates would stand if they relied on a one-sided declaration that the statutes complained of were invalid. In practice, the Confederates' dilemma was insoluble: if they insisted on full satisfaction for the claims of their church, no agreement could be made with the king; if they wanted a settlement within the existing constitutional framework, they must be satisfied with such conditions as they could induce the king to grant; and though political necessity drove Charles to make large concessions, both the same necessity, and his own conscience, made it impossible that he should consent to what the nuncio and the bishops demanded—the establishment of Roman Catholicism 'in as full lustre and splendour as it was in the reign of King Henry VII, or any other Catholic king',[48] with all the rights of authority, jurisdiction, and property that this implied.

This dilemma split the Confederates into two groups: one, led by the Old English nobility and gentry, advocated peace with the king on the best terms available; while the other, supported by most of the clergy and the native Irish, advocated active prosecution of the war until their full claims had been satisfied. The division was reinforced by economic considerations. The Old English leaders were anxious for the security of their estates, and since they had suffered comparatively little in earlier confiscations, they were more concerned about guarantees for the future than about restitution for the past. In the religious settlement, the benefits they particularly looked for were a guarantee of practical toleration, and admission to public office; and since many of them held monastic property, they feared that if the clergy were made too powerful they might demand the restoration of secularized church lands. The native Irish (and more particularly those of Ulster) who had lost much, or all, of their estates by successive confiscations, were correspondingly less cautious in their policy, and more exacting in their demands, so that they had a natural bond of union with the clergy. They opposed the 'Ormond peace' of 1646 not only because its religious terms were condemned by the ecclesiastical authorities, but also because it held out no hope that they would recover their own, or their ancestors', estates.

This party conflict, nourished on religious and racial animosity, bred a bitterness which has sometimes infected even historians of the period. But the bitterness must not be allowed to hide the fact that the Confederates as a whole stuck to the principles with which they set out. Though each party accused the other of treachery, to church or crown as the case might be, each repudiated the charge, and protested loyalty to both. It is not, of course, surprising that the Old English, while defying the censures of the bishops, should insist on their loyalty to the church; but it is easy to overlook the fact that the native Irish, while refusing to come to terms with Ormond, were equally insistent on their loyalty to the king.[49] The difference between the parties was one of emphasis, not of principle; of means, not of ends. Neither thought of separating Ireland from the crown of England, neither aimed at a constitutional revolution, and neither could conceive of any final settlement except in alliance with the king. The conflict that split the Confederates was in some measure a continuation of the long-standing struggle between the Old English and the native Irish, and in some measure a struggle between the secular and the ecclesiastical power,[50] but it was not a struggle between 'nationalist' and 'anti-nationalist' forces.

The conflict of opinion between Old English and native Irish naturally extended to questions of military policy. Contemporary commentators and later historians, hostile to the Old English, have accused them of lukewarmness and even duplicity in the conduct of the war, and have censured them for their readiness to negotiate with Ormond. It seems desirable, therefore, to offer some comment on the relation between the policy of the Confederate government and the course of military operations.

Less than one-third of the period from December 1641, when the recusants of the pale joined the Ulster insurgents, to January 1648/9, when the Confederation was formally dissolved, was occupied by active warfare between the Confederates and the royal government in Dublin. A cessation of arms for one year, concluded in September 1643, was followed by negotiations for a definitive peace, and was extended from time to time until peace was publicly proclaimed in July 1646. This proclamation precipitated a clerical *coup d'état* in Kilkenny, and the new Confederate government formed by Rinuccini resumed hostilities with Ormond. But it was not long before fresh negotiations were on foot, and these continued intermittently until the eve of Ormond's departure from Ireland, after handing over Dublin to the commissioners of the English parliament, in July 1647. They were taken up again on Ormond's return in September 1648 and issued in the peace of January 1648/9, the terms of which included the formal dissolution of the Confederation.

Some modern historians, from Meehan onwards, have criticized this policy of negotiation, on the ground that the Confederates, if they had pressed on with the war instead of making a truce, would have won a speedy and decisive victory. Donelan, in his essay on the Confederation already referred to, writes as follows:[51]

> The Confederates failed to take the tide of victory when it served, and wasted their time in futile negotiations with a man who certainly had not the power, even if he had the will, to grant them what they haggled for.

But the interpretation of the period presupposed in such criticism is open to serious objection. In the first place, the constitutional position taken up by the Confederates compelled them to seek an understanding with the king; this, and not a military victory over the royal forces, was their main purpose. For them to reject an opportunity of negotiating would be directly contrary to their own repeated declarations of policy.[52] It is true that within the Confederation itself the cessation of 1643 aroused some controversy, and was opposed by Scarampi, the papal envoy, and by some at least of the native Irish. But the importance of this opposition must not be over-emphasized. Scarampi was not a Confederate, his interests were purely ecclesiastical, and he was not concerned about the royal cause save as its fortunes might affect his church. For our knowledge of the attitude of the native Irish leaders we are largely dependent on the 'Aphorismical discovery', and the chief arguments there put forward against the cessation are that Ormond was really in league with the English parliament, and that to come to terms with him was to betray the interests of the king. To blame the Confederates (as Meehan, for example, seems inclined to do) for not taking the opportunity to destroy completely English power in Ireland, is to blame them for not acting contrary to their own professions, or, we might perhaps say, for belonging to the seventeenth century instead of to the nineteenth.

Even from a purely military point of view, it may be questioned whether the Confederates were in a position to win a decisive victory in the summer of 1643. They were certainly stronger than they had been a year earlier, and Ormond was desperately short of men, money and supplies: both these points were stressed by Scarampi in his case against the cessation, and there is a good deal of other evidence to the same effect.[53] Ormond's weakness prevented his maintaining the offensive, though he made a temporarily successful incursion into King's County in July;[54] but it does not follow that the Confederates could have driven him out of Dublin. Sir John Temple, master of the rolls and a member of the Irish council, who opposed the cessation, thought their position very precarious: 'the rebels are almost starved and worn out in Ulster, beaten in Munster, and in great want of munition in Leinster'.[55] The ill-success of the Confederate armies in 1644 and 1645 suggests that Temple's estimate may not have been far wrong.

The cessation neutralized the armies under Ormond's command, and left the Confederates free to deal with the Scots and parliamentary forces in Ulster, who rejected the cessation from the beginning, and with Inchiquin, who transferred his allegiance to the English parliament in 1644. But in fact the Confederates accomplished almost nothing. By June 1644 Owen Roe O'Neill had been, to use his own words, 'driven' into Louth, 'by the invincible power and force of the Scots in the north';[56] and Castlehaven's expedition into Ulster later in the year, which was intended to restore the position, ended in fiasco. In 1645 Castlehaven gained some initial successes in Munster, but failed completely to dislodge Inchiquin. Coote's capture of Sligo, opening the way into Connaught, more than counterbalanced all that the Confederates had gained since the cessation.[57] It would be rash to conclude from this that the Confederates, if they had continued the war in 1643, would have had no chance of a speedy victory; but there is little reason to regard it as inevitable, and certainly not enough evidence to justify Butler's sweeping statement that 'they could easily have conquered all Ireland and then made their own terms with Charles'.[58]

Whatever chance the Confederates may have had, in 1643, of bringing the war to a rapid and successful conclusion did not recur. By June 1644 they were appealing, almost desperately, to Rome for money and military equipment; and in August, De la Monnerie, French agent at Kilkenny, in a report to Cardinal Mazarin, declared that the Confederates were so short of supplies that if the truce ended, and they had to fight Ormond as well as the Scots and parliamentarians, they would be unable to sustain the struggle without powerful foreign protection.[59] Even O'Neill's great victory at Benburb, in June 1646, had a merely negative effect on the military position; it prevented the Scots from marching south to attack Kilkenny, but it did not open the way for a general Confederate victory. This negative character of what appeared at first to be a decisive success, has been commonly attributed to the lack of unity among the Confederates themselves.[60] Lack of unity certainly had a disastrous effect on Confederate strategy; but it does not wholly explain O'Neill's failure to follow up his victory. This was due also to military considerations: the Scots forces in Ulster, even in defeat, were too strong to be ignored,[61] and O'Neill was in no position to bring them to another engagement; though he had replenished his supplies with the spoils of battle, he was still short of equipment and money. Within eight weeks of Benburb he was writing to Ormond: '. . . as for my part, I protest before God I know not how or which way I could at the present time bring one hundred men to a head, for want of means or provision.'[62]

By this time, in any case, the failure of the king's cause in England had decisively altered the whole situation in Ireland. Whether or not the Confederates had lost a chance of imposing a settlement by force in 1643, the dilatoriness of their negotiations with Ormond during the succeeding years certainly destroyed their chance of gaining one by agreement. By October 1644 the Supreme Council admitted that the king had already promised 'as much as is reasonable for us to demand in temporal matters, either for the freedom of the nation or the assurance of . . . estates', but they still held out for better terms in religion:[63] yet they accepted the peace of 1646, which did not give them any-thing more, in principle, than they might have had two years earlier. A junction of forces between Ormond and the Con-federates, which Rinuccini was able to prevent in 1646, was still possible in 1644, and would have changed the whole course of the war, not only in Ireland, but also in Great Britain. The really damaging criticism of the Confederate's policy is not that they preferred negotiation to fighting, but that in their negotiations they refused to face the realities of the situation. Scarampi had warned them, in July 1643, that if parliament were victorious, their cause would be ruined.[64] He had used this as an argument against making a truce with Ormond, and in this respect the Confederates may have been justified in ignoring it; but the warning was soundly based, and they should have realized that having decided to agree with their adversary they must do so quickly.

The political and military ineptitude of the Confederates opened the way for the Cromwellian conquest, the catastrophic effect of which serves to underline the magnitude of their failure. But despite this failure, the Confederation is a significant land-mark in Irish history. In it was first established, though imper-fectly, a fusion of Old English and native Irish on the basis of a common faith and a common allegiance to crown and constitu-tion. By the reign of James II the fusion was virtually complete, and the principles of Kilkenny had a brief triumph in the 'patriot parliament'. Not until the nineteenth century did they once more enter the field of active politics, and contribute to the complicated pattern of modern Irish nationalism.

NOTES

1. C. P. Meehan, *The Confederation of Kilkenny* (Dublin, 1846).
2. *A contemporary history of affairs in Ireland from 1641 to 1652*. . . . *With an appendix of original letters and documents*, 3 vols. (each in two parts) (Dublin, 1879–80) (hereafter referred to as *Contemp. hist.*); *History of the Irish Confederation and the war in Ireland, 1641–1649* . . ., 7 vols. (Dublin, 1882–91) (hereafter referred to as *Confed. and war*).
3. *Commentarius Rinuccinianus de sedis apostolicae legatione ad foederatos Hiberniae catholicos* . . ., 6 vols. (Dublin, 1932–49) (hereafter referred to as *Comm. Rin.*).
4. Special reference may be made to the work of the Rev. D. F. Cregan (*Irish historical studies*, ii. 394–414), and the Rev. Professor P. J. Gorish (ibid., vi. 83–100, viii. 217–36; *Irish theological quarterly*, xviii. 322–7, xxi. 32–50, xxii. 49–57). The Rev. D. F. Cregan's un-published thesis, 'The Confederation of Kilkenny: its organization, personnel and history' (National University of Ireland, 1947), con-tains a very valuable account of the Confederation's governmental system.
5. It cannot be said that this need has been met by Professor T. L. Coonan's *Irish Catholic confederacy and the puritan revolution* (Dub-lin, London, New York, 1954); see review in *Irish historical studies*, xi. 52–5.
6. E.g. 'His majesty's Catholic forces for the province of Munster' (Terms of surrender of Askeaton Castle, 14th Aug. 1642, in *Confed. and war*, ii. 51).
7. Cf. *O.E.D.*, s.v.
8. *Confed. and war*, ii. 320.
9. For the form of the oath of association see *Confed. and war*, ii. 210–12; and cf. D. Coffey, *O'Neill and Ormond*, pp. 238–40.
10. The terms 'native Irish' (sometimes 'old Irish' or 'ancient Irish') and 'Old English' were regularly used by contemporaries, including the Confederates themselves. It might be argued that by the mid-seventeenth century the distinction that they indicated had become, through frequent intermarriage, one of politics rather than descent; but in so far as surnames are a guide to descent the distinction between the two main groups among the Confederates had some national basis in fact as well as in terminology. There were, of course, some exceptions: Lord Muskerry (Donough MacCarty) always acted with the Old English, and might, for all practical purposes, be reckoned as one of them.

11. See the contemporary accounts of the proceedings of the recusant lords and gentry of Leinster, 1641–2, in *Confed. and war*, i. 268–88, 299–301.

12. Acts of the General Assembly, Oct. 1642, in *Confed. and war*, ii. 80.

13. Acts of the congregation at Kilkenny, May 1642, in *Confed. and war*, ii. 36, 37.

14. Ibid., i. 112.

15. R. Bagwell, *Ireland under the Stuarts*, ii. 26.

16. It is, in fact, so described in Stephen Gwynn, *History of Ireland*, p. 292.

17. *Confed. and war*, i. 87, 111.

18. The Supreme Council consisted of twenty-four members, but business was normally conducted by twelve 'residents', three from each province; the quorum was nine, and the concurrence of at least seven was necessary to the validity of any act. (Acts of the General Assembly, Oct. 1642, in *Confed. and war*, i. 75–6.)

19. Acts of the General Assembly, Oct. 1642, in *Confed. and war*, ii. 80.

20. Numerous examples of orders issued by authority of the Supreme Council both to provincial commanders and to subordinate officers will be found in *Calendar of the state papers relating to Ireland . . . 1633–47* (London, 1901), e.g. pp. 374–5, 429, 430, 441, 469, 478, 479–80, 635, 674, 693.

21. *Comm. Rin.*, i. 314–19.

22. *Confed. and war*, ii. 37.

23. Ibid., ii. 83.

24. Declaration of Bishop John Burke, of Clonfert, 2nd Mar. 1642/3 (ibid., ii. 219–21).

25. G. Davies, *The early Stuarts, 1603–1660* (Oxford, 1937 (The Oxford history of England)), p. 86.

26. S. R. Gardiner, *History of England, 1603–42* (1883–4), x. 92 n.

27. J. Nalson, *Impartial collection of the great affairs of state, 1639–49* (1682), ii. 555–7.

28. *Cal. S.P. Ire., 1633–47*, pp. 347–8.

29. *Desiderata curiosa Hibernica* (Dublin, 1772), ii. 78, 83.

30. Ibid., ii. 111–12.

31. The motto inscribed on the Confederates' seal was 'Pro Deo, pro rege, pro patria Hibernia unanimis'. (*Cal. S.P. Ire., 1633–47*, p. 336; *Confed. and war*, i. preface, p. lxv.)

32. *Confed. and war*, i. 236.

33. Reprinted ibid., iii. 336–9.

34. Ibid., i. 245, 265–7; ii. 49.

35. 16 Car. I, cc. 33, 34, 35, 37; cf. *Commons' jn.*, ii. 425; Gardiner, *History*, x. 173.

36. *Commons' jn., Ire.*, i. 290–1, 303–5; *Cal. S.P. Ire., 1633–47*, pp. 303, 315.

37. *Commons' jn., Ire.*, i. 313, 319, 348, 374, 399, 400, 407.

38. *An argument delivered by Patrick Darcy, Esquire; by the express order*

of the house of commons in the parliament of Ireland, 9 Iunii, 1641.
(Reprinted, Dublin, 1764.)

39. *Confed. and war*, ii. 141–3, 238; iii. 130, 286–7, 303, 310–11.
40. E.g. in 'Articles of cessation of arms. . . .' (ibid., ii. 365–76), signed by Muskerry and eight other representatives of the Confederates.
41. See, e.g. R. Dunlop, *Ireland from the earliest times to the present day* (Oxford, 1922), p. 105; cf. same author in [old] *Cambridge modern history*, iv. 525.
42. Answers made by the Confederates' commissioners to Ormond's demands, Sept. 1644 (*Confed. and war*, iii. 321–2).
43. 'An explanation of some of the answers given in the behalf of the Confederate Catholics of Ireland . . .' (ibid., iv. 243).
44. Cf. Castlehaven (*Memoirs* (ed. 1680), p. 23): 'If a letter came to them [the Supreme Council] written in Irish, it would be wondered at; and hardly could one be found to read it'.
45. 'A remonstrance of grievances in the behalf of the Catholics of Ireland . . .' (17th Mar. 1642/3), in *Confed. and war*, ii. 238.
46. Ibid., ii. 131.
47. Ibid., ii. 212; *Comm. Rin.*, ii. 510 ff.
48. The first 'proposition' of Jan. 1646/7 (*Comm. Rin.*, ii. 510 ff.).
49. Cf. O'Neill to Ormond, 13th Oct. 1648, 24th Sept., 1st Nov. 1649 (*Contemp. hist.*, i. (pt. 2). 751; ii (pt. 2). 276–7, 314).
50. Apart from the major conflict over the terms of peace, there were disputes over episcopal appointments, in which the Supreme Council wished to have the same sort of influence as had been exercised by the crown before the reformation (see, e.g. Supreme Council to Wadding [28th June 1643], 13th June 1644 (*Confed. and war*, ii. 277–8; iii. 182–4)), and over monastic estates in lay hands. Perhaps the most dramatic clash of lay and clerical claims was the attempt to arrest Bishop MacMahon in Nov. 1647 (Bagwell, *Stuarts*, ii. 160–1, and authorities there cited).
51. J. Donelan, 'The Confederation of Kilkenny', in *Studies in Irish History, 1603–1649* (ed. R. B. O'Brien), pp. 321–2.
52. Cf. The reasons for the cessation, sent by the Supreme Council to Luke Wadding, at Rome, 1 Oct. 1643: 'It was the king's pleasure, whose rights and prerogatives we have sworn to maintain, that there should be a cessation of arms.' (*Confed. and war*, iii. 23–4.) For a discussion of Wadding's attitude to the negotiations see Fr. Canice Mooney, O.F.M., 'Was Wadding a patriotic Irishman?', in *Father Luke Wadding commemorative volume*, ed. by the Franciscan fathers, Dun Mhuire, Killiney (Dublin, 1957).
53. *Confed. and war*, ii. 321–7; lords justices and council to Lenthall, 11th July 1643, same to Nicholas, 9th Sept. 1643 (H.M.C. *Ormonde*, New Series, ii. 297, 309).
54. T. Carte, *History . . . of James, duke of Ormonde* (1736), i. 439–40.
55. Temple to Rev. Thomas Temple, 16th June 1643; cf. same to earl of Leicester, 20th June 1643 (*Confed. and war*, ii. intro., pp. xlvi–xlviii, l–liv). Temple's evidence might be suspected on the ground that the

E

parliamentary party in England, which he favoured, opposed the cessation as likely to strengthen the king. But Temple was in Dublin at the time, and must have believed that the city could hold out until help arrived. The uncertainty resulting from conflicting arguments over the policy of cessation is well summed up by E. Borlase (*History of the . . . Irish rebellion* (1680), p. 134): 'To what party the cessation was happy will be hard to determine.'

56. O'Neill to Ormond, 17th June 1644 (*Contemp. hist., i* (pt. 2). 588–9).
57. Carte, *Ormonde*, i. 515–16, 528–9; Castlehaven to Supreme Council, 17th June 1645 (*Confed. and war*, iv. 281–7); Bagwell, *Stuarts*, ii. 59–60, 90–3, 95–6.
58. W. F. T. Butler, *Confiscation in Irish history* (Dublin, 1917), p. 120.
59. *Confed. and war*, iii. 190–4, 263–4.
60. See, e.g. E. Curtis, *History of Ireland*, p. 248.
61. Bagwell, *Stuarts*, ii. 121.
62. O'Neill to Ormond, 25th July 1646 (*Contemp. hist., i* (pt. 2). 690).
63. Supreme Council to Wadding, 26th Oct. 1644 (*Confed. and war*, iv. 35–6).
64. *Comm. Rin.*, 413–20.

Four

The Irish Viceroyalty in the Restoration Period

IN 1660 someone transcribed into the 'Town Book' of Belfast a copy of 'Verses presented to General Monck':

> *Advance, George Monck, and Monck St George shall be,*
> *England's restorer to its liberty,*
> *Scotland's protector, Ireland's president,*
> *Reducing all to a free parliament;*
> *And if thou dost intend the other thing,*
> *Go on, and all shall cry God save the king.*[1]

The last two lines reflected the outlook of most Irish protestants in the early months of 1660; and though there was some republican sentiment in the army, it was too ill-organized to be effective. Ireland was, in fact, ahead of England in readiness to bring the king home; and it was mainly the fear of offending English opinion that dissuaded Charles from going there first. But though the pattern of restoration was very similar in both kingdoms, and though in each it brought a revival of old constitutional forms, there was a profound difference between the general attitude prevailing in England and that which characterized those who organized and supported the restoration in Ireland. In England, there was a widespread and genuine, if rather naïve, belief that things could go back to what they had been before the civil war. Among Irish protestants the restoration of the monarchy was regarded as the best guarantee for the preservation of the great change in the balance of power and property that had taken place as a result of the Cromwellian conquest, confiscation and plantation.

The expectations of the Irish protestants were substantially fulfilled. Despite the element of compromise in the acts of settle-

ment and explanation the greater part of the landed property of
the kingdom remained in their hands; and their control of the
municipal corporations was confirmed. When parliament met,
in 1661, it was, for the first time, a purely protestant body. Under
the early Stuarts the Roman Catholics had still enjoyed a share
of political power, though it was a share much smaller than their
numbers and wealth would have warranted; but this power, lost
under the Cromwellian régime, was not recovered at the Restoration. The 'protestant ascendancy', which was to establish itself
fully in the next century, had already made good its exclusive
hold on the constitutional system. But this ascendancy was not
yet secure. The Roman Catholics, it is true, were little likely to
risk a new insurrection; but they had not given up hope; their
influence at court was considerable, though fluctuating; and they
looked forward, not without reason, to some radical change in
royal policy that would give them back all, and more than all, that
they had lost in the wars of the mid-century. Not until this
prospect had been half realized and then finally blasted in the
events of the Revolution could the protestants feel that their
ascendancy was fully and safely established. From this point of
view the period of the Restoration may be seen as an uneasy
interval in the great struggle for power that dominated the political life of Ireland in the seventeenth century. This characteristic
is one of the factors that give special interest to the study of
Anglo-Irish relations during the period.

The Irish protestants, who were mostly of English descent,
had long formed an important link between the two kingdoms,
and their increase in numbers and wealth during the Cromwellian
period strengthened that link. There were, besides, many Englishmen, from the duke of York downwards, who, though they had
not themselves settled in Ireland, had acquired a direct interest in
Irish property. It was, perhaps, even more important that the
events of the 1640s had suggested the possibility that the fate of
protestantism in England might depend, in the long run, on its
fate in Ireland. Altogether, then, it is hardly surprising that the
English parliament, and English opinion generally, now took a
more continuous interest in Irish affairs than had been usual in the
earlier part of the century. It is worth noting also, though it may
be no more than a coincidence, that it would be hard to find any
earlier period in which so many men of Irish origin appear among

the important figures in the political life of England. Ormond and Orrery, Ranelagh and Conway, would all count in English politics, even if one were to ignore their activities in Ireland.

It is not only, however, the condition of Ireland that gives a special interest to the study of Anglo-Irish relations at this period. The state of affairs in England is hardly less important. Charles had to struggle almost continuously (at least down to 1681) to preserve his independence of action against encroachment by the house of commons or domination by his ministers; and in this struggle Ireland was a not unimportant factor, both for its own sake and as a potential source of money and troops. Inevitably, then, the rival political groups, engaged in almost ceaseless conflict for office and influence, fought hard to gain or to retain the management of Irish affairs. In all this there was, no doubt, an element of financial greed as well as political ambition: Ireland offered rich pickings to politicians and their friends, and even the privy council clerks competed for the 'agency of Ireland' and the perquisites that it carried.[2] But, despite all this, the struggle over Irish government was at bottom a political struggle; and at its centre was the office of viceroy. It is in the status of this office, and in the conditions of its tenure, that the character of Anglo-Irish relations can most readily be traced.

It is important, in the first place, to remark on a significant change in the kind of man to whom the government of Ireland was entrusted. The viceroys of the early Stuarts were administrators, royal servants whose importance derived from the office that they held. Even Wentworth is hardly an exception to this rule, for he had neither following nor influence except as a minister of the crown. But the viceroys of the Restoration period were all, at the time of their appointment, established political figures, who might expect to carry some weight in the world, quite apart from the influence attached to their office. Albemarle received the viceroyalty, in the summer of 1660, as part of the reward for his great services to the monarchy; but he had no intention of going to Ireland, and less than two years later he was succeeded by Ormond, whose influence dominates the history of Ireland and of Anglo-Irish relations for almost half a century. On Ormond's removal, early in 1669, the king appointed Lord Robartes, who seems to have accepted the office with reluctance and who certainly laid it down with alacrity nine months later, when he was succeeded by

Lord Berkeley of Stratton. Though neither Robartes nor Berkeley equalled Ormond in personal influence, both (and especially Robartes) were men of some independent political importance; and the same is true of Essex, who succeeded Berkeley in 1672 and held office for five difficult years. Ormond, reappointed in 1677, was still in office when Charles II died. But his recall had already been decided upon; he left Ireland in February 1685; and before the end of the year the new king's brother-in-law, the second earl of Clarendon, was appointed to succeed him. It is not unworthy of remark that, whereas the viceroys of the earlier part of the century had ruled Ireland as lord deputies,[3] all these men held the more dignified title of lord lieutenant. The change of practice might mean little or nothing in terms of actual power; but it is indicative of the new importance attached to Ireland and its government.

In these circumstances it was impossible for a viceroy to avoid becoming involved in the cross-currents of English politics. It is, of course, true that earlier viceroys had, from time to time, been similarly involved; but what had formerly been occasional or incidental now became regular and vital. Throughout the Restoration period the appointment of a lord lieutenant, his security in the office and his final recall were more often and more directly influenced by the state of conflicting groups and policies at court than by regard for the immediate problems of Irish administration. This is not to say that Irish considerations were wholly ignored; but they had little independent force; they might be brought in, by one party in the conflict or the other, to support (and sometimes to camouflage) a line of action determined upon for quite different reasons. How these various interests and influences affected the situation can be seen in the circumstances surrounding the removal of the duke of Ormond, in February 1669, and the appointment of his successor.[4]

In constitutional theory the viceroy depended wholly and directly on the king; but the king was bound to be influenced by those around him, and, in practice, no viceroy could be safe if he were faced by the hostility of the dominant faction at court. In these circumstances, the fall of Clarendon, in August 1667, carried with it a threat to Ormond's position: the two had been closely associated, and those who had overthrown the chancellor were anxious to get rid of his allies also. The king himself recognized that Ormond might well feel uneasy, and wrote to assure him of his undiminished regard, whatever 'malicious people' might say to the contrary.[5] There is no reason to doubt the sincerity of this assurance; but when the ex-chancellor wrote to Ormond ten days later his tone was more sombre: 'God preserve you and yours and keep your master firm to you, for I believe I have few enemies who do not desire to oblige you the same way they have done me'.[6] There is implicit in the contrast between these two letters a question that was to take sixteen months in answering: was the king's personal regard sufficient to protect his representative against a determined attempt by a powerful court faction to unseat him?

It might seem, at first sight, that the question has been stated in over-simple terms. For one thing, Charles's support was seldom very reliable; for another, the enemies of Clarendon were not, at least to begin with, firmly united against Ormond: Arlington, in particular, was disposed to assist him so far as he could do so without danger to his own position or prospects. But there is no evidence to suggest that Charles, left to himself, would have made any change in the viceroyalty at this time; and Arlington's rather ambiguous help, though it may have delayed the final issue, did not save Ormond. In the long run, what mattered was the weight of pressure brought upon the king to act against his own original inclinations. In the building up of this pressure Buckingham took a leading part: not only did he regard Ormond as his enemy, but he wished either to succeed to the government of Ireland himself or to have it placed in the hands of a dependable ally. His first design was to use his influence in parliament. Articles were prepared for an impeachment of Ormond; and men who had specific grievances against his administration were encouraged and supported in presenting petitions for redress to the house of commons.[7] But Ormond did not suffer from that general unpopularity which had made Clarendon so vulnerable; and the prospects of success in parliament were, at the least, doubtful.[8] It might, however, be easier to make out a case against Ormond's financial administration; and Anglesey, the vice-treasurer, was already being closely questioned about his accounts.[9] Any prospect of an increase in revenue would appeal to the king; and it was no doubt with this possibility in mind that Buckingham turned for help to Orrery, whose long experience of Irish affairs entitled him to speak with authority, especially in matters of finance.[10]

Orrery received Buckingham's advances very cautiously. It was not until March 1668 that he made up his mind to go to London; and even then he had not finally committed himself: his correspondence with Ormond at this period shows how ingeniously he was trying to keep a foot in either camp.[11] Ormond himself, of course, was well aware of the moves against him and was at this time weighing up the advantages and disadvantages of going to court to defend his position.[12] He had received the king's permission to do so as early as February 1668,[13] but he still hesitated; and it was almost certainly his suspicion of Orrery's purpose that finally decided him to make the journey. He reached London in May; and Orrery, who had been held up by an attack of gout, followed him in June.[14]

After a fortnight in London Ormond summed up his prospects, as he saw them, in two sentences. In a letter to his eldest son, Ossory, now his deputy in the government of Ireland, he wrote:

> The king seems well satisfied with the account I gave him of the management of his affairs, and not at all disposed to take them out of my hands. But if the faction against me should prevail in the parliament, it is not sure, but it must upon him.[15]

It was a reasonable assessment of the position. Though parliament had been prorogued ten days earlier, it was expected to reassemble in the course of the summer; and Ormond, with Clarendon's fate before him, might naturally assume that the king would find it almost impossible to resist a demand by the house of commons for his removal. In fact, parliament did not meet again until after the issue had been decided; and yet, even so, its influence on the outcome cannot be wholly ignored: Buckingham's determination to get rid of Ormond was strengthened by the fear that failure to do so would damage his own prestige and thus weaken his influence with the house of commons. In spite of all his efforts, however, almost nine more months were to pass before he gained his end.

At first, things went well for him. Orrery, now openly critical of Ormond, put forward evidence about the revenue and expenditure of Ireland that seemed to indicate mismanagement in the past and to promise a surplus for the future. The effect was twofold. First, a proposal for summoning an Irish parliament to grant additional revenue—a proposal that might well have meant keeping Ormond in office—was now dropped. Secondly, a committee of inquiry was set up; and of this committee Buckingham was the most prominent member. The committee, though it failed to fasten any direct responsibility on Ormond himself, did find fault with the financial administration and heavily censured his vice-treasurer, Anglesey. To this extent, at least, Ormond's position was weakened. But the result of the committee of inquiry, by itself, was indecisive.[16] The main threat to Ormond now came from another quarter.

Since the beginning of Buckingham's attack Ormond had relied on the help and advice of Arlington, who, as Ossory's brother-in-law and close friend, was unwilling to appear openly against him.[17] But Arlington had his own interests to look to; and by the autumn of 1668 he seems to have decided that his future lay in a close alliance with Buckingham. There is almost certainly some connexion between this decision and a proposal that Arlington put before Ormond in November: Ormond was to retain the lord lieutenancy, but remain in England, and the government of Ireland was to be entrusted to three lords justices, of whom Ossory was to be one.[18] Ormond, though he expressed no distrust of Arlington's sincerity, saw the proposal simply as a first step towards his complete removal; and he refused to co-operate.[19] It is likely that the king would have been glad of some such settlement, which would have satisfied, or partly satisfied, the Buckingham faction, without putting upon Charles himself the ungrateful task of dismissing an old servant in whom he had so often declared his confidence. Indeed, once Arlington and Buckingham were united in working for Ormond's removal the only barrier that remained was Charles's reluctance to come to the point of decision. Even at this stage, the barrier was difficult to surmount; and it was not until 14th February 1669 that Charles announced in council that Ormond was to be relieved of the government of Ireland and Lord Robartes appointed in his place.[20]

Out of all this emerge several important points. First, the threat to Ormond did not arise from any weakness in his administration or from any change in royal policy, but from a shift in the balance of influence at court. Those who worked for his removal certainly made use of complaints against his government and endeavoured to persuade the king that a change would be in the royal interest; but their motives had little to do with either the prosperity of Ireland or the welfare of the monarchy. The vice-royalty of Ireland was too important a post to be left in the hands of a potential enemy; and Ormond in office was dangerous as a potential rallying point for Buckingham's enemies. Ormond himself told Arlington, in November 1668, that the desire for his removal 'did not arise from my conduct in Ireland, but here'; and he was met by the significant reply that he was over-familiar with men who were unfriendly to Buckingham.[21]

Secondly, we must not regard the king's ultimate surrender as an indication of the weakness of the crown, of an inability to resist a demand put forward by powerful ministers and advisers. Undoubtedly, Charles was under very heavy pressure from men whose support he wished to retain and whom it might, perhaps, have been dangerous to alienate; but he would never have yielded if he had had any real interest in holding out. Ten years later, during the 'Popish Plot' crisis, when Ormond, then recently restored to the government of Ireland, was under far heavier and more widespread attack than in 1668–9, Charles resisted every demand for his removal, because he was convinced that Ormond's services were essential to the safety of the monarchy.[22]

Thirdly, Charles's surrender in 1669 was, after all, only half a surrender. If the removal of Ormond was a concession to Bucking-ham and his associates the appointment of Robartes as his successor represented the king's own choice and yielded them neither satisfaction nor advantage. As Ormond wrote to Lord Chancellor Boyle, 'I am persuaded some men who have laboured hard to effect this change do meet with as much mortification and disappointment as they designed me'.[23]

It is at least possible that the appointment of Robartes was in-tended as something more than a demonstration of the king's independence in the choice of an Irish viceroy. It may also have represented a move in Charles's current policy of conciliating the presbyterians and preparing the way for some measure of religious toleration. There is a hint of this in the account of the whole transaction sent by Peter Talbot to the nuncio at Brussels. Talbot was ill-informed about the details; but he was in London at the time, and he at least knew the reputations of those involved. He has this relevant comment on Lord Robartes: 'vir est sagax necnon severus, sed assertor libertatis conscientiae quamvis vulgo putetur presbyterianus'; and he makes it clear that from his viewpoint Robartes was more acceptable than Ormond.[24] The choice of a crypto-presbyterian viceroy who would yet meet with even qualified approval from an ecclesiastic of Talbot's standing among the Irish Roman Catholics, would certainly have been in line with Charles's policy at this time. But whatever Charles's motives may have been, the whole transaction, from the fall of Clarendon in August 1667 to the removal of Ormond in February 1669, serves to illustrate the position of the viceroyalty both in relation to the crown and in relation to the political factions that strove for influence in parliament and at court.

There are some obvious similarities between this campaign against Ormond and the series of attempts to secure the removal of Essex, attempts which began within two years of his appointment in May 1672 and continued, almost without intermission, until his recall five years later.[25] The same methods were used against him: pressure on the king, charges of mismanagement, encouragement of complaints from Ireland. But, despite these similarities, the circumstances were, in one important respect at least, very different. The attack on Ormond had been, in origin, personal; as an ally of the ex-chancellor and as a potential (if not actual) danger to the dominant faction he must be driven from power. The attacks on Essex, though not uninfluenced by personal ill-feeling, were actuated by the desire to put the management of Irish affairs into other hands. Ormond had one set of enemies; and the campaign against him was a single operation consistently pursued. Essex had to face the hostility of various groups and individuals who, for one reason or another, desired a change in the government of Ireland. For more than three years he had to struggle against enemies who were sometimes in alliance against him, sometimes at odds among themselves, sometimes even disposed, for the time being, to support him. His most constant and most baffling difficulty was to know whom he could trust and whom he must watch with caution.

Among those who attacked Essex were royal favourites and other hangers-on of the court, who resented his refusal to cooperate in their plans for the plundering of Ireland: he had difficulty, for example, in keeping the Phoenix Park out of the grasp of the duchess of Cleveland.[26] But he despised such 'little people', as he called them. They were a source of annoyance rather than a serious threat; they might join in cabals against him, but their enmity was unlikely to decide his fate. His real danger lay in the fact that Irish affairs had become a factor in the struggle for political power; and all his efforts to stand aside and keep 'the plain way' were unavailing.

At the time of Essex's appointment the Cabal was on the brink of dissolution, and Sir Thomas Osborne (or, to give him the name by which he is most commonly known, the early of Danby) was rising steadily in influence. With his nomination as treasurer, in June 1673, he assumed first place among the king's advisers. But this did not give him the monopoly of influence at which he aimed; he was jealous of all rivals; and, in particular, he resented Arlington's continuation in office as a secretary of state. It was because of this tension between the treasurer and the secretary that Essex first became dangerously, and unwillingly, involved in the struggle for power at court. In accordance with his formal instructions he maintained a regular correspondence with Arlington, though he also corresponded with the treasurer on financial matters. But Danby wished to bring the whole business of Ireland under his own control, thus extending his influence at Arlington's expense. This was not a matter that he could put openly before Essex; but he made no secret of his views; and his complaint on the subject to Conway, in November 1673, was probably intended to be transmitted to the lord lieutenant, as it almost immediately was:

> Lord Treasurer told me that Essex was so locked up in a box with Arlington that he could entertain no correspondence with Essex but civility. My answer was, that Essex entered not into any intrigues with Arlington but only transmitted affairs by Arlington to the king; he replied that that was Arlington's greatest support.[27]

This last statement may well contain some exaggeration; but it cannot be lightly dismissed. To Arlington, fighting to retain office, every shred of influence was important; and at this time the king had good reason to be specially concerned about Irish affairs. By the terms of a contract concluded in August 1671 Lord Ranelagh had undertaken to manage the finances of Ireland: he and his partners were to collect the payments due from the farmers of the revenue and to meet all the charges, including arrears, upon the Irish establishment, both civil and military.[28] Ranelagh did not fulfil his obligations, and his accounts were never cleared; but there can be no doubt that large sums were paid privately to the king, who thus had an interest in the maintenance of the 'undertaking' and in frustrating any attempt at a detailed investigation. In these circumstances, then, Arlington's control of Irish correspondence may well have been an important source of strength to him. That he himself considered it in this light is strongly suggested by his displeasure, in April 1674, when he conceived that Essex had ignored him by approaching the king directly on a question concerning grants of land; and it was only with some difficulty that Essex's agent in London, William Harbord, was able to smooth things over.[29]

Danby was not so easy to satisfy as Arlington. Essex replied at once, via Conway, to the complaint of November 1673, justifying his conduct on the ground of the king's instructions, but expressing himself in conciliatory terms:

> Pray acquaint your friends that upon all occasions of the revenue I shall not fail to communicate them to my lord treasurer; for matters of grants to my lord keeper; and for other intelligence, by the king's especial command, I am to apply to my lord of Arlington.[30]

Conway, still in the guise of a friendly mediator, returned to the question in the following May. This time the complaint was a specific one: Essex had written to Danby 'to quicken Ranelagh in his payments, for otherwise Essex should be obliged to make a representation of it', when, in fact, the representation had already been made, through Arlington and without a word to Danby, two weeks earlier.[31] Once again, Essex sent a prompt reply, answering the particular charge against him and explaining, at greater length than before, the principles on which he conducted his correspondence with England.[32] But neither excuse nor explanation was relevant to the real issue. Conway's letter was, in effect, a letter of warning: it is significant that before opening the subject of Danby's complaint he impressed upon Essex the hopelessly friendless position in which Arlington now stood. The core of his message lay in a single sentence: 'If your excellency will take my word for it, you cannot split upon any other rock than by running a tilt at Ranelagh and by being thought too much of a party with Arlington'.[33]

The introduction of Ranelagh's name in this context is very important. Less than four months after the date of Conway's letter Arlington was finally obliged to give up the secretaryship; and this event might appear to open the way for a better understanding between Danby and Essex: they had, in fact, exchanged formal professions of friendship some weeks before Arlington had actually resigned office.[34] But, even if Danby could have overcome his suspicion of Essex, engendered during the previous twelve or fifteen months, his close alliance with Ranelagh made friendly co-operation with Essex almost impossible. It was Essex who had to face, in Ireland, all the ill-effects of Ranelagh's failure to keep his engagements: a perpetual shortage of money, growing arrears, an unpaid army; while Ranelagh, fertile in excuse and in the manipulation of accounts, parried all Essex's complaints, and was protected by the treasurer, as well as by his own influence with the king.

This state of affairs did not by itself constitute an immediate threat to Essex's tenure of the viceroyalty. Neither Danby nor Ranelagh was ready with a candidate for the succession; and their relations with Essex were outwardly correct and even friendly. But his knowledge that they were likely to join in any move that might be made against him added to the difficulty of his position; and in the repeated calculations of his prospects that occupy so much space in the correspondence of his agents in London they are always figures of ill-omen. 'About eight of the clock', wrote William Harbord on 26th June 1675, 'I went to the king's bed-chamber and there found keeper, treasurer, Lauderdale, Conway and Ranelagh and that they had gotten king into a corner and were very busy with him and were speaking about parliament and Essex.' It was a typical scene, in essentials if not in detail; and Essex's friends at court had a hard task in looking after his interests. On this particular occasion Harbord and Sir Henry Capel called in the help of Coventry, whom they found 'nodding in his office' at three o'clock in the morning; and between them they foiled the attempt that the others were making to render Essex's proposed visit to London impossible.[35] But, though the visit was successfully made, Essex had hardly returned to Dublin before his enemies were at work on further plots against him. And yet, despite all these threats to his position, despite Danby's influence, Ranelagh's money, Conway's treacherous ingenuity, despite the prestige of Monmouth, whom they brought into their schemes, Essex survived until, in April 1677, Ormond's long patience under royal disfavour was at length rewarded by his restoration to the government of Ireland.[36]

At first sight, there might seem to be an obvious parallel here with the events of 1667–9; it might seem that Charles was once more demonstrating his unwillingness to be hustled by his advisers and his reluctance to dismiss a faithful servant. But, though the parallel is not without value, the differences between the two situations are more striking than the similarities. Essex was under attack for a much longer period than Ormond had been; he was not, like Ormond, attached to the fortunes of a fallen minister; and, though his family's sufferings in the royal cause certainly entitled him to consideration, he himself could hardly bear comparison with Ormond in either length or value of service. It is, therefore, not altogether unreasonable to seek some further explanation of the king's tardiness in making a change in the vice-royalty at this time; and such an explanation can be found in the condition of contemporary Scotland.

During the whole period between the Restoration and the Revolution the Scottish government was kept in a state of alarm by the activities of the covenanters. The problem that they posed was of more than merely Scottish interest. Throughout the British Isles the authorities were nervously alert to every rumour of movement among 'fanatics' of all descriptions; and reports of collaboration between Scottish covenanters and malcontent puritans, however improbable such collaboration may in fact have been, were seriously received. In these circumstances, the position of Ireland was of particular importance. On the one hand, the existence of a strong colony of Scottish presbyterians in Ulster, separated only by the narrow waters of the North Channel from the main headquarters of the covenanters in Galloway, exposed Ireland to the dangerous infection of covenanting principles; and it was feared that if an insurrection in Scotland met with any initial success it would be followed by a sympathetic movement among the Irish presbyterians. On the other hand, Ireland had a standing army, which might, in an emergency, supply a force that could be quickly transported to the south-west of Scotland, where insurrection was most likely to break out.[37]

It is not clear when the idea of using Irish troops was first put forward; but the decision to do so was communicated to Essex in June 1674.[38] He received his formal instructions in August; and in October a 'brigade' of 1,600 foot and four troops of horse was stationed on the shores of Belfast Lough, ready for transport to Scotland when called for.[39] In fact, no call came; and the 'brigade' was broken up twelve months later.[40] In June 1676 Essex was instructed to prepare a similar force; but on this occasion the period of service was much shorter: the 'brigade' seems to have been broken up before the end of the year and, once again, without having been sent for out of Scotland.[41]

For two-and-a-half years, then—from the summer of 1674 to the end of 1676—the possibility of using Irish troops in Scotland was almost constantly in the air; and for about half that period an expeditionary force was actually in being, ready to sail. Its efficiency would depend very much on the viceroy, who was at the head of the military as well as of the civil establishment; at such a time there was little to be said for replacing Essex by some nominee of the Danby–Ranelagh faction. It is significant that no change was made until the king had at length determined on a full reconciliation with Ormond, who had a respectable military reputation; and it was made at a time when Lauderdale was seemingly convinced that he could suppress the covenanters without seeking help from outside Scotland. To say that Essex's survival in office had depended solely on the crisis in Scotland would be an obvious exaggeration; but to ignore that crisis and its influence on the position in Ireland would be at least equally misleading.

The accounts here given of the removal of Ormond in 1669 and of Essex in 1677 indicate clearly enough the difficulties and dangers of the viceroy's position. In principle, he was safe so long as he retained the king's confidence, a point upon which both Ormond and Essex repeatedly insisted; but, in practice, he could not rely on that confidence surviving the attempts of his enemies to undermine it; and such enemies, even if they could not convert the king to their point of view, could yet make the viceroy's position extremely uncomfortable.

It might be said that every great officer of state was in much the same sort of situation: his tenure depended on his retaining the confidence of the king; and he had constantly to defend himself against the machinations of his rivals. But the viceroyalty was in some ways unique: it carried with it responsibility for a whole kingdom; its holder was of necessity entrusted with a good deal of discretionary power; it involved prolonged absence from court. Ideally, perhaps, it might have been left completely outside the area of English political conflict; but, in fact, the affairs of the two countries were so closely intertwined that such separation was impossible. Every major political development in England had its echo in Ireland; and whatever group was, for the time being, dominant in the direction of English policy had to take account also of the government of Ireland.

These circumstances placed the viceroy in a position of peculiar difficulty and peculiar danger. The difficulty lay in his being, of necessity, a court politician *in absentia*, dependent upon allies and agents in London to keep him accurately informed of the situation there, to warn him of likely developments and, on all matters of dispute, to present his case not only to the king but to others whose support might be won or whose enmity might be averted. For these services, Ormond relied especially on his son, Ossory, and after Ossory's death, on Sir Robert Southwell; Essex relied constantly on his brother, Sir Henry Capel, and from time to time on secretaries—William Harbord, Francis Godolphin and Sir Cyril Wyche; Clarendon, in James II's reign, relied almost exclusively on his brother, Rochester. The peculiar danger to which the viceroy was exposed, and against which his English agents were expected to protect him, lay in the fact that his authority in Ireland rose or fell with Irish opinion of his standing at court. It was of great importance to him, therefore, that he should be seen in Ireland as the sole channel of communication with the crown, that no petitions should be received at court unless forwarded through him, that all appointments, all grants of land or money, in short, all marks of royal favour, should be received at his hands and not as a result of direct application to England. This was, indeed, the accepted mode of procedure; but its neglect was one of the most frequent sources of complaint from the viceroys of the period; and the complaint was particularly bitter when the favour granted was one that the viceroy was known to oppose. In one such case, Essex put the viceroy's position very forcibly in a letter to his brother:

> If you did but know with what contempt and scorn my Lord Berkeley was used by all people here after they found he was not supported at court, it would not be thought strange if I have a

F

more than ordinary concern at these things, which seem so little in themselves; for indeed the nature of this people is very apt to trample on their superiors; and unless a man be thoroughly countenanced in England there is no dealing with them.[42]

A consideration of the difficulties that faced a viceroy of Ireland at this period, the almost ceaseless battle for survival that he was forced to wage, the humiliations to which he was liable to be exposed, might make one ask why any man should accept, much less seek, such an uncomfortable office, which, along with all its other disadvantages, involved exile from the centre of power. That it ranked as one of the highest posts open to a subject might satisfy ambition, and that it offered a unique opportunity to serve the crown might appeal to loyalty; but the most obvious, and most readily measurable, attraction of the viceroyalty lay in the emoluments attached to it. These, though they cannot be stated with precision, were very considerable. The viceroy's allowances on the military list amounted to more than £11,000; he received almost £7,000 more in other regular payments; fees on licences for the export of wool (one of the perquisites of the office) yielded, in the 1670s, between £3,000 and £4,000 a year.[43] Though the expenses necessarily incurred by a viceroy were high, this income left room for a substantial surplus. Essex, though determined to govern honestly, certainly regarded the viceroyalty as a means of repairing his fortunes; in discussing the prospect of buying Essex House, he reckoned on being able to set aside, for that purpose alone, £2,000 each half year.[44] Carte, indeed, asserts that Ormond, as viceroy, spent more than he received; but the duke's notion of what was required of a viceroy who was also head of the house of Butler would probably have taxed any income. And even for Ormond the viceroyalty had a financial importance, at least in the 1660s: the large sums of money due to him by the terms of the Restoration settlement, which were hard enough to collect even while he was in office, might well prove irrecoverable under an unsympathetic successor.[45]

One must remember, also, that the viceroyalty carried with it a great deal of patronage, especially in the army and in the church; and a viceroy could do much to advance his allies and dependants: to be appointed one of his chaplains was a long step towards the episcopal bench. In the ill-defined area that separated this regular patronage from corrupt practice the viceroy could be very useful to those who enjoyed his favour, as, for example, in disputes (very frequent at this time) over grants of land. Only one viceroy of the period, Lord Berkeley, was seriously suspected of actual corruption; and it is doubtful if the charge could be made good against him personally, though his secretary, Sir Ellis Leighton, by whom he allowed himself to be guided, was certainly involved in a conspiracy to cheat the citizens of Dublin over their water supply.[46] It is, naturally, impossible to assess the patronage and influence attached to the viceroyalty in financial terms; but they certainly enhanced the value of the office, and, even when confined within the limits of seventeenth-century honesty, they formed a not unimportant element in the return it yielded to its occupant. Yet, when all this has been said, when every allowance has been made for the attraction of a large income and an opportunity of advancing one's friends, these considerations alone do not explain the almost unceasing struggle over the viceroyalty that marked the Restoration period. What was at stake was not private profit but political power, a controlling influence in the direction of royal policy. The government of Ireland might not be a major factor in the situation, but it was too important to be ignored; and those who aspired to control the affairs of England must make sure, if they could, that Ireland was in friendly hands. In the Restoration era, not for the first time, and certainly not for the last, Ireland proved to be a complicating factor in the politics of England.

NOTES

1. R. M. Young (ed.), *The Town Book of the corporation of Belfast, 1613–1816* (Belfast, 1892), p. 79.
2. Sir Robert Southwell to Ormond, 7th Feb. 1680 (H.M.C. *Ormonde*, New Series, iv. 578–9); Francis Gwynn to Ormond, 7th Feb. 1680 (ibid., v. 271).
3. Mountjoy, lord deputy at the accession of James I, became lord lieutenant in May 1603 and retained the title until his death; but, during this period, he was an absentee and Ireland was governed by lord deputies. Wentworth was appointed lord lieutenant in Jan. 1641 (sworn in, 18th Mar.); but he left Ireland early in April and never returned (F. M. Powicke and E. B. Fryde (ed.), *Handbook of British Chronology* (2nd ed., 1961), pp. 158–9).
4. So far as the sequence of events is concerned the following account of Ormond's removal is based mainly on Thomas Carte, *Life of*

James, First Duke of Ormonde (3 vols., London, 1735–6), ii. pp. 346–78.

5. Charles II to Ormond, [13th] Sept. 1667 (Carte, *Ormonde* (London, 1735–6), ii. p. 353). Throughout this paper, dates are given in new style for the years, in old style for the days of the month. Spelling and punctuation of passages quoted have been modernized.

6. Clarendon to Ormond, 24th Sept. 1667 (ibid., ii. appendix, p. 38).

7. Carte, *Ormonde*, ii. p. 356–60.

8. Note, for example, the failure of Wheeler's attack on Ormond in the house of commons in Mar. 1668 (ibid., ii. p. 364).

9. Ormond to Ossory, 24th Jan. 1668 (ibid., ii. appendix, pp. 51–2); ibid., ii. p. 365.

10. Ibid., ii. p. 365. Carte asserts that Buckingham induced the king to write an encouraging letter to Orrery, lest the latter should fear to take sides against the lord lieutenant. But the letter itself (ibid., ii. appendix, p. 50) gives no direct support to this statement: it is dated 30th Nov. 1667 and is simply an assurance that Orrery will not be adversely affected by 'the late change' (i.e. the dismissal of Clarendon).

11. Ormond to Orrery, 10th Mar. 1668; Orrery to Ormond, 13th Mar., 17th Mar. 1668 (Carte, *Ormonde*, ii. appendix, pp. 55, 56, 58–9).

12. Ormond to Ossory, 12th Nov. 1667, 24th Jan., 25th Feb. 1668 (ibid., ii. appendix, pp. 44–5, 51–2, 54).

13. Ormond to the king, 4th Dec. 1667 (H.M.C. *Ormonde*, New Series, iii. pp. 281–2); the king to the lord lieutenant, 7th Feb. 1668 (*Cal. S.P. Ire., Ire, 1666–69*, pp. 572–3).

14. Burghclere, *Ormonde*, ii. pp. 146–7.

15. Ormond to Ossory, 19th May 1668 (Carte, *Ormonde*, ii. appendix, p. 60).

16. Carte, *Ormonde*, ii. p. 369. A statement of income and expenditure in Ireland between 1660 and 1667, apparently drawn up in Anglesey's defence, shows a heavy deficit: during the period the total of the sums 'received out of England' exceeded £200,000 (Trinity College, Dublin, MS. F. 2.1). Cf. *Cal. S.P. Ire., 1666–69*, pp. 257–9.

17. Ormond to Ossory, 30th June 1668 (Carte, *Ormonde*, ii. appendix, p. 62).

18. Same to same, 21st Nov. 1668 (ibid., ii, appendix, pp. 66–8). The proposal seems to have originated with Orrery, who took credit for having won Arlington over by this device (A. Browning, *Danby*, ii. p. 22).

19. Carte, *Ormonde*, ii. pp. 373–4.

20. Ibid., ii. pp. 375–6.

21. Ormond to Ossory, 21st Nov. 1668 (ibid., ii. appendix, p. 67).

22. Ibid., ii. p. 492.

23. Ormond to Boyle, 8th Mar. 1669 (ibid., ii. appendix, p. 70). Cf. Duchess of Ormond to ——, Feb. 1669 (H.M.C. *Ormonde*, New Series, iii. p. 442).

24. Talbot to nuncio, 15th Feb., 25th Feb. 1669 (P. F. Moran (ed.) *Spicilegium Ossoriense*, i. pp. 470–1).
25. Some aspects of Essex's viceroyalty are dealth with in Clement E. Pike, 'The Intrigue to Deprive the Earl of Essex of the Lord Lieutenancy of Ireland', in *Trans. Roy. Hist. Soc.*, Third Series, v (1911). pp. 89–103.
26. Essex to Francis Godolphin, 7th Mar. 1673 (O. Airy (ed.) *Essex papers*, i. p. 58).
27. Conway to Essex, 15th [misprinted 18th] Nov. 1673 (ibid., i. pp. 139–41).
28. R. Bagwell, *Ireland under the Stuarts*, iii. p. 119.
29. Harbord to Essex, 14th Apr. 1674 (O. Airy (ed.), *Essex papers*, i. p. 212).
30. Essex to Conway, 29th Nov. 1673 (ibid., i. pp. 143–4).
31. Conway to Essex, 19th May 1674 (ibid., i. pp. 228–9).
32. Essex to Conway, 26th May 1674 (ibid., i. pp. 231–4).
33. Conway to Essex, 19th May 1674 (ibid., i. pp. 228–9).
34. Essex to Danby, 14th Aug. 1674 (ibid., i. p. 249).
35. Harbord to Essex, 26th June 1675 (C. E. Pike (ed.), *Essex Letters*, ii. pp. 33–5).
36. Carte, *Ormonde*, ii. pp. 463–4.
37. On the general character of the situation see J. C. Beckett, 'Irish-Scottish relations in the seventeenth century', in *Transactions of the Belfast Natural History and Philosophical Society*, 1964, pp. 38–49. Above, pp. 26–46.
38. Sir Arthur Forbes to Essex, 27th June 1674 (B. M. Stowe 205, f. 272).
39. Same to same, 17th Aug., 23rd Aug. 1674 (ibid., ff. 394, 409); same to same, — Oct. [endorsed 'Rec. Oct. 22'] 1674 (B. M. Stowe 206, ff. 127–8).
40. The king to Essex, 27th Sept. 1675; Forbes to Essex, 16th Oct. 1675 (B. M. Stowe 208, ff. 305, 339); Essex to lords justices of Ireland, 28th Oct. 1675 (*Letters written by . . . earl of Essex . . . 1675* (Dublin, 1770), p. 345).
41. Coventry to Essex, 10th June, 13th June 1676 (B. M. Stowe 209, ff. 336, 350). The subsequent history of this 'brigade' is obscure; but that it was broken up before the end of 1676 may be inferred from the terms of Danby's letter to Lauderdale, 15th Sept. 1677 (Browning, *Danby*, ii. p. 47).
42. Essex to Sir Henry Capel, 9th May 1674 (O. Airy (ed.), *Essex papers*, i. p. 224).
43. For payments on the military list see *Cal. S.P. Ire.*, *1666–69*, pp. 68–9; *1669–70*, p. 8. For other regular payments see H.M.C. *Ormonde*, New Series, vii. pp. 172–3. For income from wool licences see ibid., iv. 665 ff. (and cf. L. M. Cullen, *Anglo-Irish trade, 1660–1800* (Manchester, 1968), pp. 35–6).
44. Essex to Sir Henry Capel, 16th May 1674 (O. Airy (ed.), *Essex papers*, i. pp. 226–7).

45. Carte, *Ormonde*, ii. p. 364; Ormond to Ossory, 27th Nov. 1667 (ibid., ii. appendix, p. 47).
46. Essex to Arlington, 22nd June 1673 (O. Airy (ed.), *Essex papers*, i. pp. 103–4); R. Bagwell, *Ireland under the Stuarts*, iii. pp. 99–101.

Five

The Government and the Church of Ireland under William III and Anne

THE difficulties and problems which the revolution of 1688 presented to people of tender conscience were, in England, smoothed over and covered by circumstances. The king's flight left the tories free to frame, at least for their own consumption, a theory which secured to them the benefits of revolution without the sin of rebellion. The anglican church itself, than which no institution had more openly maintained the doctrine of non-resistance, found that the accomplished fact could be accepted with a face-saving show of consistency; even the moral and intellectual eminence of the non-jurors failed to secure more than a handful of followers for their schism.

In Ireland, on the other hand, it was impossible to escape or gloss over the issues involved. With King James actually in the country there was no half-way house between submission and rebellion. The established church especially was in a position of great delicacy, for the policy of James II had resulted in separating the English interest from the royal interest in Ireland. The church, traditionally attached to both, was in a dilemma. Clarendon, lord lieutenant at the beginning of James's reign, foresaw the danger and warned the king of it.[1] The warning was un-heeded and Tyrconnell completed the breach. To support James now meant to support a new state of affairs in Ireland, based upon complete toleration and partial establishment for the Roman Catholic church, which was already being subsidized out of the revenues of the vacant bishoprics,[2] and upon the overthrow of the existing land-settlement. To resist meant rebellion. But hesitating Irish protestants were troubled by a practical as well as a moral problem. To resist might not merely be sinful, it might also be unsuccessful; resistance without William's help

87

was bound to fail, and while William's attitude remained doubtful the possibility of coming to terms with James was not lost
sight of.[3]

Even after the issue of the war in Ireland had resolved these
doubts, it was necessary to justify the transference of allegiance
from James to William. The work was done by William King,
who had been dean of St. Patrick's before the Revolution, and
earned the bishopric of Derry by his *State of the protestants of
Ireland* no less than Walker did by his share in the defence of the
city. King's argument, stripped of non-essentials, is simply this:
that the government of James II threatened the established church
in Ireland with extinction, and that to resist was not rebellion but
self-preservation. That this view was held almost universally by
Irish protestants is clear from the fact that the Irish church came
through the revolution without a schism. But this seeming unity
was a sign of weakness rather than of strength. Its source was not
in any organic or spiritual unity, but in the dependence of the
church on the protestant landowners and on the English interest
in Ireland. To trace the attempts made during the reigns of
William and Mary and of Anne's to restore the church to something more like an independent position is the purpose of the
present essay.

At first sight, indeed, it might seem strange that the church survived the revolution with its privileges intact. The protestant
dissenters were quick to claim credit for the prompt and effective
support which they had given to William's cause. Throughout
Ireland they expected a legal toleration, and in Ulster they seem
to have hoped to share the success of their brethren in Scotland
and establish presbyterianism in the place of episcopacy.[4] While
the issue of the war was still uncertain William gave some encouragement to these hopes by renewing and doubling Charles II's
grant to the presbyterian ministers of Ulster, the *regium donum*.[5]
A general religious settlement of Ireland, however, was postponed,
and this postponement, as much as anything else, saved the
establishment. William's peaceful succession in England and the
conquest of Ireland enabled the Irish church to return to its
former position as ally of the royal influence and the English
interest in Ireland. This alliance tended to identify the interests
of the established churches in the two kingdoms; and when, in
Nov. 1690, a committee was appointed to consider the state of

religion in Ireland, it was a committee of English churchmen, who might be relied upon to support the existing order.[6]

It was, indeed, the fact that the church formed part of the existing order that helped it to survive: in Ireland as in England the continuity of the ecclesiastical organization tended to disguise the magnitude of the changes which had taken place. The war of the revolution had shown the Irish landlords how completely their position depended on English help. In Ireland they could ally themselves neither with the presbyterians nor with the Roman Catholics. The former were too independent; the latter were not yet reconciled to the new state of affairs, nor hopeless of changing it.[7] But if the system of minority rule was to be maintained without open reliance on the armed force of England, the landlords must find some other sanction for it. They found it in the maintenance of the exclusive right of members of the established church to political power, a principle which received its strongest expression in the imposition of the sacramental test in 1704.

This close alliance with the landlords is the basis of the church's political influence during the eighteenth century. It explains the rapid recovery, after the shock of the revolution, which enabled the church to have the question of a legal toleration for protestant dissenters shelved in 1692 and again in 1695. The attitude of Sir Richard Cox, one of the justices of the common pleas and a member of the privy council, is typical of his class. His opposition to toleration cost him his seat on the council, and writing of his dismissal a few years later he said: 'I was content every man should have liberty of going to heaven, but I desired nobody might have liberty of coming into government but those who would conform to it'.[8]

Such a purely negative policy, however, was not likely to satisfy those clergy who wished to see the church strong enough to fight her own battles, without relying too much on English government or Irish landlords. As Archbishop King put it in 1715: 'The bulk of the common people in Ireland are either papists or dissenters, equally enemies to the established church: but the gentry are generally conformable, and the church interest apparently lies in them'.[9] But at the same time he had little hope of getting anything to the benefit of the church from the landlords' representatives in parliament without some corresponding effort by the clergy themselves.[10] He and others like him hoped to strengthen and extend the church by a policy of reform. Their failure to secure parliament's co-operation in this increased the desire of some of them to recover the church's power of reforming itself without reference to parliament.

To begin with, most of those who supported a policy of reform regarded it not only as good in itself, but as a means by which the church could regain its proper authority. Bishop Foy of Water-ford, one of the most indefatigable of reformers, wrote: 'We have but a shadow of discipline left which cannot be exercised without the concurrence of the state.' The conclusion he draws is that the clergy must by their learning and piety acquire influence over their flocks to take the place of compulsion.[11] Till the clergy had reformed their own ranks this was little likely to happen.

There were two principal and closely related abuses against which Foy and many others strove for years—pluralities and non-residence. Pluralities (that is the holding of two or more benefices by a single clergyman) were commoner in Ireland than in England, partly because they were not restricted by law,[12] partly because of the poverty of Irish livings. Pluralities meant non-residence, for pluralists had no objection to distance. Dr. John Bolton, for example, when appointed to the deanery of Derry, wished to continue to hold the vicarage of Laracor (county Meath), assuring King that this would not prevent his residence in Londonderry.[13]

Reforming bishops had two remedies for these problems. As an immediate measure they insisted that where an incumbent could not himself reside he should provide properly for the serving of the parish. As a real cure for the evil they wished so to increase the value of livings that the excuse for pluralities would disappear. The poverty of the livings was genuine enough, and was largely due to the impropriation of the tithe to laymen. In the diocese of Meath, for example, of fifty-nine rectories forty-two were im-propriate, twenty-four of them to one man.[14] In describing the diocese of Ferns, King wrote: 'I find the clergy very regular and diligent, but in a most miserable condition as to their maintenance. Some have eight, nine, nay ten parishes and not forty pounds per annum out of them.'[15]

These problems were not new and were dealt with by existing canons. The difficulty was to see that the canons were enforced.

'It is not an act to authorize us we stand in need of', wrote Foy, 'but to force and constrain as likewise to prescribe the manner how it is to be performed.'[16] Bishop King found that his clergy in Derry paid little attention to existing canons: 'I am in ill circumstances here, my absentees and pluralists care not whom they employ, and therefore take Scotch curates, as gentlemen used to take Irish servants merely because cheaper than others. Five pound in the salary would prefer a Turk to the best man'.[17]

At first the tendency of these reformers was to look to the state for assistance. In a series of letters to King, Bishop Foy comes back again and again to this point. For example, the government had had to instruct Primate Boyle to hold a meeting of bishops to discuss bills necessary for the church before the next parliament; a change of ministry in England was likely to help the church interest; the government must assist in preventing the promotion of unsuitable clergymen.[18] In these projects for enlisting the support of the state, the reformers got little encouragement from the primate, who probably realized better than his younger subordinates the dead weight of opposition to reform, both within and without the church. In June 1691 he warned King against allowing his zeal to carry him too far.[19] In October of the same year, in reply to King's complaints about the activities of dissenters in the diocese of Derry, he wrote rather half-heartedly: 'I shall endeavour (as far as God shall enable me) to perform those services to the church which the condition of these times will give us any encouragement to expect or hope for'.[20]

So slight appeared the chances of inducing the primate to take any lead in the move for reform that the reforming bishops in Ireland tried to make use of the royal authority to compel him to act. Bishop Dopping of Meath drew up a letter on the subject of pluralities and non-residence; the lords justices were then persuaded to forward this to the king, to be sent in his name to the primate, ordering him to take these problems into consideration.[21] Nothing came of this move, and shortly afterwards the bishop of Meath was dismissed from the council, which left the church poorly represented there.[22] Thus the chance of direct encouragement for the reformers from the Irish government was reduced. On the other hand, it does not appear that the English government was opposed to reform. So long as the prerogative was respected, William was little inclined to meddle personally in church affairs,

but was content to leave them to the queen and the bishops. It was
here that the Irish reformers found their opening, and almost
every scheme which they put forward was explained beforehand
to the archbishop of Canterbury and often to other English
bishops as well.[23]

Why was it that with this direct and indirect support from
England and with the alliance, already referred to, between the
church and the Irish house of commons, so little was done for the
cause of reform? There are two answers. First, though the commons were prepared to defend the exclusive privileges of the
church, as they did in 1692 and 1695, they represented the class
most interested in maintaining lay impropriations, and most
closely allied with that section of the clergy who benefited by
pluralities. King's early attempts to reform the diocese of Derry
were hampered by clergy of this sort—'slugs of seven or eight
hundred pounds a year', Foy called them. 'For, say they, take
away pluralities, and the gentle easy way of getting livings, and
wherein doth the church differ from a conventicle?'[24] The landlords were prepared to defend the church but not to reform it at
their own expense nor at the expense of their relations. All this is
clearly expressed in a letter from the primate to Bishop King:

> Your lordship I find in one part of your letter seems to depend
> upon some redress from me in the matter of pluralities and non-
> residents; as to the first, my lord, I am clearly of opinion that they
> are founded upon a law wherein the king, the nobility, and
> amongst them your lordship, and many other persons of the best
> quality are interested, and such as are so supported I do not see
> how they can be avoided, and to be free with your lordship I do
> not think fit especially at this time to contend with the preroga-
> tive or justle with the laws in that point, lest a worse thing
> happen to the church than it may be your lordship is at present
> aware of.

With regard to non-residents the existing laws should be enforced
'and if those laws be in any wise defective we must wait with
patience till a further law can be obtained'.[25] Secondly, as this
letter sufficiently indicates, the church was not itself at unity on
the question of reform. No one realized more clearly than the
reformers themselves the need for episcopal solidarity if anything
was to be accomplished.[26]

In spite of all these discouragements schemes for reform were

pressed on. Among other things, Bishop Foy was particularly
keen on instituting a fund for the purchase of impropriations.[27]
At the same time endeavours were being made to secure for the
church those impropriations which had come into the hands of the
government through forfeitures. But the basis of all these schemes
was that the government should be induced, by episcopal pressure
on parliament, on the lords justices, or on the ministry in England,
to take action for the good of the church. In 1693 Foy suggested a
meeting of bishops in Dublin to persuade the lords justices to do
something.[28] In 1698 Bishop Walkington of Down and Connor
turned for help against his rebellious dissenters to the lords
justices of England.[29] In 1697 Foy had hoped that Bishop King
and Archbishop Marsh of Dublin might be able to induce the
house of lords to bring in heads of a bill for reformation of the
clergy.[30] But the parliament of 1697 passed without anything
being done. Nor did it seem likely that anything would be done.
Even in England, church interest was temporarily on the decline.[31]
By 1697 Foy was in despair about getting any reforms for Ireland:
'I should be glad to hear if anything be likely to be done to support
our sinking church, the ruin of which I have a prospect of, and
have of a long while thought nothing but a persecution can
preserve us'.[32]

While this fruitless agitation for a general reformation was
going on, the same people were engaged in a less ambitious but
scarcely less important scheme for controlling the system by
which ecclesiastical appointments were made. Many livings were
at the disposal of bishops and private patrons, but the higher
dignities were in the gift of the crown. The reformers tried to
attack the problem both at top and bottom: that is, to keep unsuitable persons out of benefices, or if they had already been
instituted to prevent their promotion; and at the same time to
make sure that the more important appointments, especially to
bishoprics, were made with a due regard to the interests of the
church.

So far as the first of these aims was concerned, the bishops were
theoretically on strong ground, since the canon law not merely
authorized but ordered them to examine a clergyman before
instituting him into a benefice. In practice, the law was hard to
carry out without the co-operation of the government, of patrons
and, above all, of the other bishops.[33] King did refuse to institute

a clergyman presented to a crown living in the diocese of Derry; he gave as his reasons that the man's theological knowledge was insufficient, that he had previously tried to secure the deanery of Derry by purchase, and that he was living with a mistress.[34] But his action bore little fruit. The case dragged on obscurely for some time;[35] and the whole moral value of King's protest was lost when Bishop Vigors of Ferns instituted the same man into a crown living in his diocese, having found him on examination quite fit.[36]

The suggestions for checking the promotion of unsuitable persons might seem to have more hope of success. In 1692 and 1693 Bishop Foy brought forward at least four different methods by which such promotions could be prevented.[37] But the very number of the remedies proposed seems to indicate the desperate nature of the disease rather than any expectation of effecting a cure. Certainly none of Foy's plans was carried out, and promotion continued to go by interest instead of by merit.

At least one reason for the failure of these plans for controlling admission to and promotion in the church was the generality of their application. Any proposal to supervise all ecclesiastical appointments touched too many interests to be easily put into force. But individual appointments could be dealt with on their merits, and it was here that the reformers had most chance of success. Naturally they were chiefly concerned about the filling of vacant bishoprics. Here they were dealing directly with the government, and private interests, though often powerful, were not decisive. The vacancies existing after the revolution were filled on the advice of a committee of English divines.[38] Two years later, however, Irish opinion was regarded as the decisive factor in making appointments.[39]

As with the minor appointments, plans for setting up a permanent system of control—such as a commission of the Irish episcopate[40]—came to nothing. But while unwilling to yield the principle that the bishops should control appointments, the government by no means neglected their advice. The appointment of Dr. Samuel Foley to the bishopric of Down in 1694 was a notable success for the reformers. King recommended him to Sir Robert Southwell, Southwell conveyed this recommendation to the archbishop of Canterbury, and the archbishop of Canterbury used his influence with the queen. Such were the roundabout and uncertain ways in which the reforming party in the church secured its meagre successes.[41]

In sharp contrast with the indirect and almost hopeless methods by which Foy and his colleagues had to pursue their ends stands the one really important reform in the ecclesiastical administration of Ireland in the decade after the revolution—the purging of the diocese of Down and Connor. The significant fact about this is that it was carried out by the government, apparently on its own initiative, through an episcopal commission acting directly under the royal authority. Since before the revolution, Irish governments had been complaining of the neglect of his duties by Bishop Hackett of Down and Connor, who resided almost continuously in England from the time of his appointment in 1672.[42] In instituting a belated inquiry into the state of affairs the government was probably influenced as much by political as religious motives; for the bishop's neglect caused a great increase in nonconformity, and the diocese became, as the commissioners put it 'a key and inlet to the malcontents of Scotland', so that even the solemn league and covenant had its adherents.[43] In 1694 Bishop Hackett and some of the more disreputable of his clergy were deprived, and the diocese restored to some sort of order. Yet even in this apparently straightforward piece of work, it is difficult to follow the crossing lines of interest. The commission for the inquiry into the state of the diocese was addressed to the bishops of Meath, Derry and Dromore, or any two of them, and was executed by the two former. But though he was thus acting under the direct orders of the government and so might seem assured of it support, Bishop King felt it expedient to enlist the aid of the lords justices in preventing any pardon for the deprived bishop of Down being issued in England immediately after the sentence had been passed.[44] At the same time the ecclesiastical character of the commission was almost obscured by its dependence on royal authority. In 1698 Mrs. Hackett, wife of the deprived bishop, who had been excommunicated at the time of the inquiry, desired absolution; but King pointed out that, since in pronouncing excommunication he had been acting under special royal authority, he could remove it only by the same authority, and that nothing but a royal commission could absolve her.[45]

Thus the one real reform secured during this ten years of effort seemed to prove more clearly than ever the absolute dependence of the church upon the secular power. Sir Robert Southwell expressed it thus to King: 'Neither the church nor your lordship will be able to attain your quiet from any power on that side, but that it must depend from the power on this'.[46]

The reforming clergy were by no means satisfied with this dependence. Almost immediately after the restoration of peace in Ireland, Foy had tried to secure some sort of independent clerical action, 'I am [sure] your lordship both doth and will approve of the main design of the clergy doing somewhat of themselves towards reformation and wish with all my heart a select number of us could personally meet to adjust the expedients'.[47] But the difficult was to secure any reasonable degree of harmony among the bishops, even for such an informal meeting. During the parliamentary session of 1697 the bishops in Dublin did not even hold their customary meetings at the archbishop's house, no was there any effective committee for religion in the house of lords.[48] Another trouble was that these meetings were purely informal and possessed neither authority over the lower clergy nor power to impress the government. Bishop King hoped for something better. In 1693 he expressed his disappointment that provincial synods had not been revived.[49] Nothing was done about this at the time, though the following year Bishops Foy and Tennison both renewed the plea for closer co-operation among the bishops, apparently without effect.[50]

There was, however, one subject on which all the bishops and all sections of the clergy were prepared to unite—the defence of their privileged position against possible encroachments by the dissenters, especially the protestant dissenters of Ulster. Against them they were prepared to bring into force all the authority which the law allowed them; and it was when the secular government counteracted their measures that they began to feel the need for asserting their independence. Nevertheless, the leaders in this drive for self-government were the same people who all along were demanding reform of the church, and some control of ecclesiastical affairs. Partly this was an accident of geography. In 1694 Bishop King of Derry, Bishop Tennison of Clogher and Bishop Foley of Down and Connor were all men interested in reform, and it was in these dioceses that the number and power of the protestant dissenters were greatest. Partly, also, it was because those bishops who did their duty vigorously came most closely into contact with the rival claims and authorities of the dissenting sects. They found that the tolerant attitude of the government cut at the root of discipline. King complained to Lord Massereene: ' 'Tis a bad thing and the effect of faction that a man excommunicated for the sixth or seventh bastard shall pass for a saint because it is against his conscience to come to church and yet this or worse is the case of many in this diocese'.[51] And a year later he draws the conclusion that nothing can be done till the clergy have leave 'to meet and contrive effectual rules from time to time for the correcting the licentious and preventing growing evils'.[52]

But the very reason here urged as an argument in favour of self-government was likely to prevent it. For the English ministry, at this time predominantly whig, and the Lord Deputy Capel, were favourably disposed to the protestant dissenters, and little inclined to increase the independent authority of their enemies. Capel's opinion of King's activities is illuminating. Bonnel reported it to the bishop: 'He spoke favourably of your lordship; only said you were a little too hot, which he doubted not by that time you had been a while longer bishop would wear off'.[53] By King's 'heat', Capel no doubt meant his zeal for reconciling the protestant dissenters to the church; and in this same year King had experience of how difficult the task was going to be if the government's policy continued unchanged. To begin with, the dissenters were well organized. In his visitations he preached to them continually of the advantages of the episcopal system, but all he could report was, 'many plainly declared that they had no objection against their conformable minister, but durst not come to hear him for fear of their neighbours'.[54] The real trouble was that any serious attempt to enforce the law simply meant that the dissenters invoked the help of the government and defied his authority.[55]

King's experience was not unique. In 1699 and 1700, Bishop Ashe of Clogher conducted a correspondence with the lords justices, trying to induce them to give their authority to a proclamation forbidding presbyterian ministers to celebrate marriages. But in the end, since 'our cautious government will by no means be mentioned as approving it', the matter had to be dropped.[56] Against this, episcopal influence in the house of lords was sufficient to secure the rejection of a bill which would have released quakers

G

from the necessity for taking oaths.[57] But this was a purely negative victory; and in effect the established church was rapidly being reduced to a position in which it could neither govern itself nor effectively control the secular power in directing its ecclesiastical policy.

To escape from this position was a matter of growing urgency. A tentative step was taken in 1700 when Archbishop Marsh of Dublin decided to call a provincial synod.[58] Nothing seems to have come of this; but the move was significant, for already wider claims were being put forward. In October 1697 King had written to Foy of the necessity for a meeting of the Irish convocation, which had not met since the reign of Charles II.[59] Later in the same year he put the matter very strongly in a letter to Sir Robert Southwell:

> The first article in magna carta is that the church of England shall be free, and that freedom can consist in nothing but in choosing the ecclesiastical constitutions by which she is governed in convocations, and to give the king a power to call a certain number of divines and counsellors and by them to make or repeal canons for the church is as contrary to her liberty as it would be to civil liberty to grant such a power to the king to make or repeal laws. . . . If the church once come to have her constitutions altered without convocations, which are her legal representatives, she is no more free but an absolute slave, and our religion would in earnest be what the papists call it, a parliamentary religion, and changeable with every king's humour. . . . Convocation was the king's council for ecclesiastical affairs, but such a council as the parliament was for civil, and consequently part of the legislative power.[60]

There are two very significant things about this letter. First, it identifies the rights and position of the established church in Ireland with those of the church of England. Secondly, it is addressed to Sir Robert Southwell who was one of the English government's chief advisers on Irish affairs. King seems to recognize that the decisive factor for the church was its relationship to the English government, on which alone it could depend; for the church consisted, in Southwell's words, of 'those English protestants who have nothing on this side paradise to adhere to but old England'.[61]

But though King had thus appealed to England, the first

official move had to be made in Ireland. The Irish bishops had at last found something to unite them; and on 25th January 1699 they entered a formal protest in the journals of the house of lords against the taxation of the clergy by any assembly other than convocation.[62] The ending of the parliamentary session made any further action at this time impossible. But the protest once made was not allowed to drop, and an attempt was made to enlist the aid of the English bishops.[63] Until the Irish parliament should be called again, however, nothing could be done; and during the last two years of King William's reign, Irish influence in ecclesiastical affairs seems to have declined, whilst direct dependence on England increased. In 1701, for example, we find both churchmen and protestant dissenters in Ireland fixing their hopes upon a change of government in England.[64] The reforming bishops, meanwhile, exercised what authority they could in their visitations, and seem to have done something to restore order rather by persuasion than by force.[65]

The hopes of the church party, however, were revived by the accession of Queen Anne in 1702. In the first place, the queen was considered more favourable to the established church than her predecessor had been; a fact which sufficiently appears from the dejection of the protestant dissenters on the occasion.[66] Secondly, the new reign would probably mean a new parliament, and this would give the Irish clergy an opportunity to renew their demand for a convocation, this time in more favourable circumstances. It was over a year before any decision on the question of a parliament was reached, but in May 1703 the lord lieutenant was informed that it was intended to call an Irish parliament during the summer.[67] On learning this, all the bishops, with one exception, petitioned for the calling of a convocation at the same time. The bishops were not acting quite spontaneously, for they themselves had been addressed by some of the lower clergy then in Dublin, and it was in response to this that the bishops approached the government.[68]

The calling of an Irish convocation required two separate acts by the crown. First, to the ordinary writs summoning the bishops to the house of lords had to be appended the *praemonentes* or *praemunientes* clause; this ordered each bishop to bring with him his dean, his archdeacon, one representative of the chapter of his cathedral and one representative of the clergy of his diocese. The clergy so summoned, however, had no power to act as a convocation until a second set of writs had been issued, this time to the four archbishops, and it was by virtue of these provincial writs that the convocation was constituted as a national synod of the Irish church.

The unanimity with which the bishops supported the demand for a convocation at first sight appears surprising. In the past this demand had arisen from a desire to reform the church, and with this desire many of the bishops felt little sympathy. That a similar motive was behind the petition of June 1703 might be deduced from the important part taken in the agitation by William King, now archbishop of Dublin. Southwell seems to have regarded his insistence on the need for a convocation as one of the chief difficulties in the way of shelving the whole affair, for King, he wrote, 'is a mighty positive man'.[69] But the history of the convocation shows that not all the bishops, still less all the lower clergy, were animated by the same ideals as King. The unanimity which they displayed in demanding a restoration of their right to meet in convocation may be traced to a natural desire to assert their privileges and recover their independence, rather than to any hope that convocation would effectively remedy those abuses from which many of them benefited, or strengthen a discipline which many of them already found sufficiently irksome.

Though the bishops' petition was presented to the lord lieutenant, the decision would have to be made in England, nominally by the queen, really by the English ministry. To begin with, the latter were very doubtful. Nottingham consulted the attorney-general (Sir Edward Northey) and, supported by his opinion that the queen was not obliged to call a convocation with every parliament, declared that he thought it best 'not to try experiments in so untrodden a path'.[70] This was on 31st July 1703. But the Irish clergy were getting tired of delay, and on 10th August the lord lieutenant had another petition to forward to England, this time from the archbishops of Armagh and Dublin.[71] The petition insisted on the right of the archbishops and bishops to have the *praemunientes* clause inserted in their writs, but tried to placate the doubts of the English ministry by suggesting that even when this had been done the time of meeting of the convocation would remain at the queen's discretion. At this point the government gave in, and the bishops received their writs in the form employed in the reign of Charles II, that is with the *praemunientes* clause added.[72] These writs ordered the assembling in Dublin of representatives of the lower clergy at the same time as the meeting of parliament, but did not authorize the constituting of a convocation. So the bishops presented another memorial to the lord lieutenant, asking that arrangements should be made for the issue of the provincial writs. This was forwarded to England on 10th September;[73] but when parliament met on the 21st it had not been acted upon,[74] though elections for convocation had taken place and many clergy had come to Dublin for the opening of parliament.[75]

No further move was made until 7th October, when the bishops, urged on by the lower clergy, applied again for the issue of the provincial writs.[76] In forwarding the application to England, Southwell expressed the opinion that the writs might safely be granted, while the time of meeting was kept in the hands of the queen, who might prevent it altogether, if she chose.[77] Nottingham's reply was non-committal.[78] But the clergy were in no mood to wait. Once again the lower clergy took the lead, and induced the four archbishops to make a further demand for the provincial writs. The demand was even accompanied by a threat: 'they so much think it their right that, if denied, they will address the house of lords and will endeavour to oblige the chancellor to grant that writ, which, they say, ought always to go out with the other'. At the same time, however, they promised that if allowed to meet convocation would avoid quarrels and divisions and confine itself to a loyal address to the queen.[79] Perhaps influenced by the combined threat and promise, the government now gave in; and on 16th November Nottingham wrote to the lord lieutenant to have the provincial writs issued.[80] On 11th January 1704 convocation met, for the first time since 1666.[81]

This gradual surrender of the English government to the demands of the Irish bishops cannot be attributed solely to the high church sympathies of the ministry. Had they been genuinely interested in the welfare of the church they would have complied more speedily and more graciously. The insistence of the bishops on the loyalty of the church to the crown, and the absence of any hint that the convocation was to be used for extensive reform or for the establishment of independent control over ecclesiastical affairs, or indeed for any other purpose than the drafting of loyal

addresses, indicate that they understood clearly the real cause of
the government's hesitation, namely, the fear that convocation
would encroach on the royal prerogative. It can hardly have been
because this fear was entirely banished by the specious promises
of the bishops that the government finally surrendered. Partly the
real reason is to be found in the activities of English political
churchmen like Atterbury, who used his influence on behalf of
the Irish convocation in order to strengthen the position of the
English. But in considerable measure the surrender was due to
the strongly united action of the Irish church itself. While it had
to deal with individual bishops or small sections of the clergy the
government could afford to go its own way. But the petition of
June 1703 was a corporate act of the whole church, and as such the
government could not ignore it. In 1696 King had pointed out
that the church 'ought not in policy to be neglected, since this is
surely and apparently the strongest interest in Ireland'.[82] Many
years later he wrote, 'though the clergy and church need the
ministry's encouragement they have more need for our support,
and if we gain our people, as we set them up, so we will be able to
keep them in power'.[83] There was indeed no other interest in
Ireland on which the English government could rely. The Roman
Catholics were still a source of uneasiness; and the presbyterians
of Ulster, in spite of the favour shown to them, had been affected
by the unrest prevalent in Scotland.[84] If the church were alienated
the government would be left in an almost impossible position.
For a queen and a ministry whose natural inclinations were to
favour the church at the expense of the dissenters, the obvious, if
not the only, solution was to give way to the demands of the
bishops. But whatever the circumstances or forces which decided
the issue, in January 1704 the church found itself in a stronger
position than it had occupied for forty years, and provided with
the means both of reforming itself and of asserting its rights.

The meeting of convocation, though supported by all sections
of the church, had resulted directly from the insistence with
which a small group of reformers had pressed their demands upon
the government. Having failed to secure effective measures in any
other way, they fell back on the abstract right of the church to
legislate for itself. But in fact convocation did very little. It
effected no general reconstruction, nor did it successfully assert
its right to occupy the same relative position to crown and church

as parliament did to crown and state. During the first few months of its existence its most notable activity, after it had finished with the promised 'loyal addresses', was to prevent, by a representation of the lower house to the lords, the passing of a bill authorizing bishops to purchase glebes.[85] Though it continued to meet at intervals during the rest of the reign of Queen Anne, its only enactments were five canons, agreed upon in 1711 and printed with the royal assent in 1714. These canons did little or nothing to remedy the abuses about which so much agitation had been made. After as before the meeting of convocation the real source of authority in ecclesiastical affairs was the state; and such effective reforms as were procured during the reign of Anne were the work of parliament or of the ministry, and owed little if anything to the corporate action of the clergy.

This failure of convocation, either to accomplish immediate reforms or to establish its own authority, was due almost entirely to the folly of the clergy themselves. It soon became clear that there had been no real unity of purpose behind the movement that had persuaded the government to consent to the calling of a convocation. The genuine reformers were in a minority; and though the lower house drew up elaborate suggestions for reform, including a scheme for preventing the promotion of unfit persons, no action resulted. The true temper of the lower house is more apparent in its quarrels with the upper house, with the English bishops, with the lord lieutenant, with the house of commons, and in disputes of high and low church. King attributed these quarrels to English influence: 'The whole matter has been carried on principally by such clergymen as, having been educated in England, have taken their measures from some of the most forward in that country'.[86] He saw how dangerous such conduct could be to the church. United, no government could defy it; but, he wrote, 'a house divided against itself will be supported with difficulty'.[87]

The truth seems to be that the clergy had no heart in any action which was going to interfere with their income or their convenience. No reforms could be effective unless backed up by episcopal supervision; but, though the bishops had united in demanding a convocation, they did little to make either its authority or their own respected. In November 1712 King reported that eight of the Irish bishops were in England; in December 1712 that there was not one bishop in the province of Ulster; and in 1714 that there had not been more than one bishop at a time in that province for several years.[88] Even the old problem of appointments came no nearer solution. In November 1712 King mentioned a rumour 'that no bishopric of Ireland will hereafter be given to any educated in it'.[89] In effect the victory of 1703 was a barren one. The meeting of convocation made virtually no difference to the conduct of the ecclesiastical administration. Such power as the church still possessed to defend her privileges and to control policy did not depend upon the irresponsible conduct of a factious assembly, but upon the solid support which the Irish landlords, partly from self-interest and partly from genuine attachment, were prepared to extend.

This indirect influence was considerable. But its extent varied from time to time, and the difficulty of estimating it is increased by the fact that Ireland really had two governments, one in Dublin and one in London. We have then in the ecclesiastical administration a sort of triangle: the English ministry exercised a final and absolute authority, but its mandates had to be carried out by an Irish government which could not altogether ignore the demands of the church, especially when backed up by parliament. The events of Queen Anne's reign mark fairly clearly the bounds within which each source of authority was content or obliged to work.

The reign is divided into two periods by the establishment of a predominantly tory government in England in November 1710. In the first period the policy of the English government was in the main hostile to the church and favourable to the protestant dissenters. There were two exceptions to this. The first was the surrender over the question of convocation, which has already been dealt with. The second was the extension to Ireland in 1704 of a sacramental test such as already existed in England.[90] But though this was done by the addition in England of a clause to a bill sent over from Ireland for a quite different purpose, it is possible that the English government did not wish or expect the altered bill to be accepted by the Irish parliament. This at least is the explanation offered by Bishop Burnet.[91] Certainly the English government soon set to work to have the sacramental test repealed. From 1707 to 1709, two lords lieutenants worked for this end. When in 1708 Swift approached the government to secure for the Irish church a grant of the first-fruits and twentieth parts, it was suggested to him that the grant might be made if the church would support this policy.[92] In the same year the government intervened to prevent the enforcement of the act of uniformity against a presbyterian minister in Drogheda, though the archbishop of Armagh had himself sponsored the prosecution. Public opinion in Ireland expected that all this would be changed once the tories were firmly in power. But from 1710 to 1714 the only change they made was to drop the pressure for the repeal of the test. The Irish parliament and convocation called for repressive measures against the presbyterians, but nothing was done. In 1712 the ministry was given a further opportunity to make its attitude clear. A case similar to that of Drogheda arose in Belturbet, where the presbyterians attempted to establish a new congregation and held a special meeting of the presbytery of Monaghan there for the purpose. The whole church interest of the kingdom was aroused, and the lords justices (Sir Constantine Phipps and Archbishop Vesey of Tuam) reported 'that if such proceedings are not discountenanced, the consequence of them must be the destruction of the English church in this kingdom'.[93] By way of discountenancing them, ten presbyterian ministers involved were presented 'for holding an unlawful assembly and for endeavouring to disturb the peace and union of the corporation of Belturbet'.[94] But the tories acted just like the whigs. In 1713 they settled the whole matter by a compromise much more satisfactory to the presbyterians than to the churchmen, who tried unsuccessfully to re-open the case.[95] This negative policy was maintained till 1714, when the English government began to fall in with the wishes of their high church supporters in Ireland by suspending the payment of *regium donum*, and by preparing to extend to Ireland the operation of the schism act.

From the contrasts and similarities between the two periods of the reign, the conclusion to be drawn is that at this time both church and state were stronger in defence than in attack. The church was able successfully to resist the pressure for repeal of the test, but was unable to force from the government the support necessary to give effect to its persecuting tendencies. Yet eventually it went a long way towards bringing the tories round to its point of view, and so long as it could withstand the whigs and persuade the tories, its influence must be considerable. The English government, on the other hand, could not force its policy on the church so long as the latter enjoyed the support of the Irish landlords; but its control of the royal prerogative gave it a powerful means of restraining if not of guiding the church's actions. The third factor, the Irish government, seems to lack all consistency. The policy of the lord lieutenant was a mere reflection of that of the English ministry by which he was appointed. But when the government was in the hands of lords justices, who were often Irishmen and often high churchmen, some degree of independence can be seen; and even if the lords justices could not themselves act on the representations of the clergy, they at least reported them to London sympathetically, and backed them up by official advice.

This triple control of the ecclesiastical administration of Ireland virtually terminated with the reign of Queen Anne. The Irish church had inherited from the seventeenth century certain ideas of independence, of the divine right of the church as a corporation distinct from the state, of the spiritual duties as well as the temporal privileges of ecclesiastical dignitaries. But the driving force behind these ideas was temporarily exhausted. The reformers of the post-revolution period were the remnants of a past age, not the heralds of a new one. The strength of the church lay not in its influence over the people, but in its alliance with the landlords; its interest was political and economic, not spiritual. And this interest bound it ever more closely to England and to a whig ministry whose ecclesiastical policy was latitudinarian. At the same time, the disappearance of convocation, by depriving the lower clergy of any voice in the affairs of the church, increased the influence of the episcopate, where the English interest was steadily growing.

All these circumstances combined to make the control of the English government over Irish ecclesiastical affairs more direct and continuous. From this period we may date that close alliance of church and state which is sometimes represented as the complete subjection of the former, and sometimes as the complete identification of the two. It is this alliance that most historians have stressed as typical of the Irish church in the eighteenth century. Lecky, in particular, has shown in considerable detail the importance of church patronage in the administration of the kingdom.[96] But though the general conclusions which he and other historians draw cannot be controverted, the history of the period which we have just reviewed suggests two points which are commonly overlooked. First, the alliance of church and state did not spring spontaneously into existence at the opening of the eighteenth century; secondly, it was not entirely one-sided. It was, in fact, a compromise, and an almost inevitable outcome of the revolution. In England, parliament had got rid of the crown as a rival source of authority and was little likely to tolerate the high-church claim to be a state within a state; and if the church of England could not establish its independence, still less could the church of Ireland.[97] Between 1690 and 1714 the rival claims of church and state were put forward, one against the other, and a compromise worked out, the results of which were seen in the succeeding century. The church gave up much but not all. Supported by their allies in parliament, the clergy resisted the government's efforts to ease the position of the protestant dissenters. The toleration act of 1719 was passed only with the greatest difficulty; the attempt to repeal the test act in 1732 failed completely. The church had surrendered the claim to autonomy, allowed appointments to be governed by political and not religious considerations, became in fact a tool of the English administration in Ireland; but in return insisted successfully that the privileged position of the establishment should be maintained.

NOTES

1. *The state letters of Henry earl of Clarendon, lord lieutenant of Ireland during the reign of James the second* (ed. of 1765), i. 351–6.
2. Ibid., i. 136, 241 ff., 395–6.
3. *The state letters of Henry earl of Clarendon*, etc., ii. 324.
4. [J. Kirkpatrick,] *An historical essay upon the loyalty of presbyterians in Great Britain and Ireland from the reformation to this present year 1713*, pp. 404 ff.
5. *Cal. S.P. Dom., 1690–1*, p. 481.
6. *Cal. S.P. Dom., 1690–1*, pp. 155, 158–9.
7. Ibid., *1691–2*, p. 44. H.M.C., *Downshire*, i. pt. II, pp. 710–11.
8. *Autobiography of Sir Richard Cox*, ed. R. Caulfield (1860), p. 15.
9. R. Mant, *History of the church of Ireland*, ii. 293. The punctuation and spelling of passages quoted in this essay have been modernized.
10. Ibid., ii. 94.
11. Bp. Foy to Bp. King, 30th July 1691 (T.C.D.). Most of the letters to and from Bishop King used in this essay are taken from the originals in T.C.D. These are not bound in volumes but are arranged in boxes

according to date. Letters quoted from Bishop King's transcript-books are followed by a press-mark.

12. Bp. Foy to Bp. King, 10th Nov. 1691 (T.C.D.).
13. Bolton to Bp. King, 5th Mar. 1699[–1700], 12th Mar. 1699[–1700]; Bp. King to Bolton, 12th Apr. 1700 (T.C.D.). Cf. F. E. Ball (ed.), *Correspondence of Jonathan Swift*, 1.33 *n*.
14. Bp. Foy to Bp. King, 26th Mar. 1692 (T.C.D.).
15. Bp. King to Annesley, 3rd June 1712 (T.C.D., MS. N.3.4, pt. 1, p. 29).
16. Bp. Foy to Bp. King, 14th Oct. 1691 (T.C.D.).
17. Bp. King to Dr. Samuel Foley, 21st Mar. 1692[–3] (T.C.D.).
18. Bp. Foy to Bp. King, Aug. 1691, 19th May 1693, 8th Sept. 1693 (T.C.D.).
19. Abp. Boyle to Bp. King, 30th June 1691 (T.C.D.).
20. Abp. Boyle to Bp. King, 6th Oct. 1691 (T.C.D.).
21. Bp. Foy to Bp. King, 10th Nov. 1691 (T.C.D.).
22. Same to same, 5th Jan. 1691[–2] (T.C.D.) Bp. King to Sir Robert Southwell, 29th Apr. 1697 (T.C.D.) M.S. N.3.1, p. 65).
23. Same to same, 22nd Sept. 1691; Sir Robert Southwell to Bp. King, 15th & 17th Dec. 1691 (T.C.D.). King to bishop of Sarum, 5th Oct. 1696 (Mant, op. cit., ii. 66–7).
24. Bp. King to Dr. Samuel Foley, 7th Sept. 1691 (T.C.D.).
25. Abp. Boyle to Bp. King, 12th Jan. 1691[–2] (T.C.D.).
26. Bp. Foy to Bp. King, 22nd Sept. 1691, 8th Sept. 1693; Bp. King to Foley, 10th Mar. 1692[–3]; Foley to Bp. King, 10th Oct. 1693; Bp. Tennison (of Clogher) to Bp. King, 5th Oct. 1694 (T.C.D.; Mant, op. cit., ii. 66–7).
27. Same to same, 10th Oct. 1693 (T.C.D.).
28. Same to same, 10th Oct. 1693 (T.C.D.).
29. J. S. Reid, *History of the presbyterian church in Ireland*, ed. W. D. Killen (1867), ii. 472 ff. There is a transcript of Walkington's petition to the lords justices in P.R.O.N.I., T.525.
30. Bp. Foy to Bp. King, 10th Nov. 1697 (T.C.D.).
31. George Tollet to same, 3rd June 1696 (T.C.D.).
32. Bp. Foy to same, 1st Sept. 1697 (T.C.D.).
33. Bp. Foy to Bp. King, 14th Oct. & 10th Nov. 1691 (T.C.D.).
34. Bp. King to Dr. Dudley [?], 4th Jan. 1691[–2] (T.C.D.).
35. Bp. King to Robert King, 6th May & 26th July 1692 (T.C.D.).
36. Bp. Foy to Bp. King, 8th Sept. 1693 (T.C.D.).
37. Same to same, 26th Mar. 1692, 11th Mar. 1692[–3], 8th Sept. 1693, 10th Oct. 1693 (T.C.D.).
38. George Tollet to Bp. King, 18th Nov. 1690 (T.C.D.). *Cal. S.P. Dom., 1690–1*, pp. 155, 158–9.
39. Bp. King to Foley, 13th Sept. 1692 (T.C.D.).
40. George Tollet to Bp. King, 13th Oct. 1692 (T.C.D.).
41. Sir Robert Southwell to Bp. King, 15th May 1694 (T.C.D.).
42. Clarendon to Hackett, 25th May 1686 (*State letters of Henry earl of Clarendon* (ed. of 1765), i. 211).

43. Bishops Dopping and King to Capel, 24th Mar. 1693[-4] (*Cal. S.P. Dom., 1694-5*, p. 69).
44. Bp. King to Bp. Foley, 14th Mar. 1693[-4] (T.C.D.). See also *The argument of Archdeacon Mathews for a commission of delegates upon his appeals and querel of nullities*, 1704 (no place of publication).
45. Bp. King to Bp. Walkington, 15th Apr. 1698 (T.C.D., MS. N.3.1, p. 213).
46. Southwell to Bp. King, 1st Apr. 1699 (T.C.D.).
47. Bp. Foy to Bp. King, 29th Sept. 1691 (T.C.D.).
48. Bp. King to Bp. Foy, 28th Sept. 1697 (Mant, op. cit., ii. 94-5).
49. Bp. King to James Bonnel, 1st Dec. 1693 (T.C.D.).
50. Bp. Foy to Bp. King, 20th Sept. 1694 (T.C.D.). Bp. Tennison to Bp. King, 5th Oct. 1694 (T.C.D.).
51. Bp. King to Lord Massereene, 6th Feb. 1693[-4] (T.C.D.).
52. Bp. King to Bonnel, 4th Jan. 1694[-5] (T.C.D.).
53. B[onnel] to Bp. King, 8th Jan. 1694[-5] (T.C.D.).
54. Bp. King to Bonnel, — Apr. 1695 (T.C.D.).
55. Same to same, 10th July 1695 (T.C.D.).
56. Bp. Ashe to Bp. King, 28th Oct. 1699, 12th Jan. 1699[-1700], 24th Jan. 1699[-1700], 1st June 1701 (T.C.D.).
57. Methuen to Shrewsbury, 27th Nov. 1697 (H.M.C., *Buccleuch and Queensbury*, ii. pt. II, p. 584).
58. Sinnot to Bp. King, 2nd Apr. 1700 (T.C.D.).
59. Bp. King to Bp. Foy, 5th Oct. 1697 (Mant. op. cit., ii. 95).
60. Bp. King to Southwell, 21st Dec. 1697 (T.C.D., M.S. N.3.1, p. 149).
61. Sir Robert Southwell, to Bp. King, 26th Apr. 1699 (T.C.D.).
62. *Lords' Journ. Ire.* (1779), i. 750.
63. Bp. King to Bp. Stillingfleet of Worcester, 3rd Feb. 1699 (Mant, op. cit., ii. 100).
64. Bolton to Bp. King, 2nd Dec. 1701 (T.C.D.).
65. Bp. Ashe to Bp. King, 30th Aug. 1700 (T.C.D.). Bp. King to Abp. Marsh, 20th July 1701; to Bp. Ashe, 25th July 1701 (Mant, op. cit., ii. 105).
66. Bp. King to Bp. Ashe, 24th Mar. 1701[-2]; to Sir Robert Southwell, 28th Mar. 1702 (Mant, op. cit., ii. 124-7).
67. Nottingham to Ormond, 18th May 1703 (*Cal. S.P. Dom., 1702-3*, p. 722).
68. A summary of the bishops' petition and of the circumstances connected with it is given in *Cal. S.P. Dom., 1703-4*, pp. 8-10. A copy of the petition, with the signatures, is in T.C.D. (MS. 1.6.16), and is printed in Mant, op. cit., ii. p. x.
69. *Cal. S.P. Dom., 1703-4*, pp. 37-8.
70. Ibid., pp. 61-2, 70.
71. Ibid., pp. 86-7.
72. Ibid., p. 95.
73. Ibid., p. 112.
74. Ibid., p. 121.
75. Reeves's notes on convocation, in T.C.D., MS. 1062, p. 84.

76. Ibid.
77. *Cal. S.P. Dom.*, *1703–4*, p. 155.
78. Ibid., p. 176.
79. Ibid., p. 190.
80. Ibid., p. 204
81. Ibid., p. 494.
82. Bp. King to George Tollet, 22 Sept. 1696 (Mant, op. cit., ii. 65).
83. Same to Bp. Jenkins, 17th Feb. 1710[–11] (T.C.D., MS. N.3.11, p. 316).
84. *Cal. S.P. Dom.*, *1703–4*, pp. 229–30.
85. *Cal. S.P. Dom.*, pp. 544, 557.
86. Abp. King to Edward Southwell, 11th Sept. 1709 (T.C.D., MS. N.3.11, pp. 101–4).
87. Same to Bp. Jenkins, 20th Feb. 1712[–13] (T.C.D., MS. N.3.4, pt. 1, p. 119).
88. Same to Bp. Hartstonge of Ossory, 27th Nov. 1712; to Edward Southwell, 18th Dec. 1712; to Annesley, 3rd July 1714 (T.C.D., MS. N.3.4, pt. 1, pp. 75, 325, 311).
89. Same to Edward Southwell, 6th Nov. 1712 (ibid., p. 60).
90. 2 Anne c. 6 (*Ir. Stat.*, (ed. of 1786), iv. 23).
91. G. Burnet, *History of his own times* (ed. 1753), iv. 28–9. See also G. Simms, 'The making of a penal law, 1703–4', in *Irish historical studies*, xii. 105–18.
92. Swift to Abp. King, 28th Aug. 1708 (*Swift's correspondence*, ed. Ball, i. 105).
93. Crosslé papers (P.R.O.N.I., T.780, pp. 52–3).
94. Ibid., p. 1.
95. H.M.C., *Portland*, v. 339–40.
96. Lecky, *Ire.* (1906), i. 196 ff.
97. For an analysis of opinion in the Church of England at this period see J. C. Beckett, 'The basis of church authority', in *Theology*, liii. 163–72.

Six

Swift: The Priest in Politics

JONATHAN Swift held the deanery of St. Patrick's, Dublin, for more than thirty years; and the connexion between the man and the office became so firmly fixed in the public mind that it has survived ever since: to most people it still seems more natural to refer to him as Dean Swift than as Jonathan Swift. And yet, though we habitually use his ecclesiastical title, we are apt to forget his ecclesiastical character, or, at least, to call it consciously to mind only when something in his writings strikes us as out of keeping with his profession. But for Swift, his profession was the central fact in his life. If we often forget that he was a clergyman, he never forgot it himself, nor did he allow others to do so. There is a brief but significant passage in the *Journal to Stella*:

> Mr Secretary had too much company with him today; so I came away soon after dinner. I give no man liberty to swear or talk bawdy, and I found some of them were in constraint, so I left them to themselves.

It is probably no injustice to Swift to suggest that he was moved less by any strong distaste for swearing or bawdy talk than by a feeling that to tolerate such conversation in his presence would be to acquiesce in an insult to his office. And this feeling was not merely personal. He was constantly alert to defend the dignity of his order; and nothing enraged him more than any sign of contempt for the clergy. He himself may have hated and despised mankind in general; but he would not stand idly by while others expressed their hatred and despite of the clergy of the Church of England.

This notion of corporate responsibility lies at the heart of the subject. If we are to understand the connexion between Swift's clerical character and his political activity we must remember that as a clergyman he was an official of a great organization. It was in this way that Swift himself regarded the situation. 'I took upon myself, in the capacity of a clergyman', he wrote in his *Thoughts on religion*, 'to be one appointed by Providence for defending a post assigned me, and for gaining over as many enemies as I can'. The defence of his post involved Swift in two interlocking battles. One was against those whom he and his contemporaries called indifferently Free-thinkers, Atheists, Deists. The attacks which these writers made on revealed religion may seem to us timid, or jejune, or irrelevant, according to our viewpoints; but they appeared to Christian Europe of that day immensely dangerous, and potentially, even probably, fatal to the power of the church. Swift's second battle was in defence of the constitutional position of the Church of England, which was attacked not only by free-thinkers but by all sorts of dissenters, and even by those who professed to be its friends. It is with this latter conflict that we shall be principally concerned.

To understand Swift's part in it we must look briefly at the position of the Church of England in his day. To say that the church was going through a 'period of transition' has more meaning than is usually conveyed by that trite phrase. Even after the upheavals of the sixteenth and seventeenth centuries it still retained some traces of its former character as a self-regulating body, coterminous with the nation though not identical with it. As late as 1697 William King, an older contemporary of Swift, could write:

> The first article of Magna Carta is that the Church of England shall be free, and that freedom can consist in nothing but in choosing the ecclesiastical constitutions by which she is governed in convocations. . . . If the church, once come to have her constitutions altered without convocations, which are her legal representatives, she is no more free but an absolute slave. . . .

A few years later Gilbert Burnet stated a similar position, though only in order to refute it:

> It has passed generally among the clergy, that ecclesiastical matters could only be judged by persons deriving their power immediately from God: and as the clergy have their commission from him, so it was a received doctrine, that the king had his power likewise from God, and that therefore the church was to be governed by the king and the convocation.

By the end of the seventeenty century these views were already out of date, or, at least, they had ceased to bear much resemblance to the actual situation. They continued to be vigorously expressed; but the very notion of ecclesiastical independence, however restricted, was unpalatable to the men who moulded the opinions of the age; those who insisted on the divine authority of the church could hardly fail to perceive that the spirit of the times was against them; and the sense of defeat and frustration on the one side, and of impatience with obscurantism on the other, no doubt added to the bitterness that, in any case, seems to be an indispensable ingredient of theological controversy.

Swift must be included among those who maintained the divine authority of the church—the 'High Church' school, in the proper sense of that much-abused term. He held very clearly that the church was a divinely-instituted society, deriving its authority from Christ and the apostles, and that this authority could not legitimately be abrogated by the civil power. He based the relationship of church and state on a contract which he assumed to have taken place at the time when the state embraced Christianity; and an essential part of that contract was that the civil authorities accepted the constitution of the church, including its rights to govern itself, as a divine law, 'and, consequently, what they could not justly alter afterwards, any more than the common laws of nature'. And this, according to Swift, was precisely the position of the Church of England.

> . . . the Church of England is no creature of the civil power, either as to its polity or doctrine. The fundamentals of both were deduced from Christ and his apostles, and the instructions of the purest and earliest ages, and were received as such by those princes or states who embraced Christianity.

But though Swift thus insisted on the divine authority of the church, he recognized a practical distinction between possessing authority and possessing liberty to use it. The civil power was, in a physical sense, supreme; and it might, by force, prevent the clergy from performing any of their ecclesiastical functions, as it might prevent them 'from eating, drinking, and sleeping'; but it could not itself validly perform those functions, which Christ had committed to the church alone.

Swift never organized his ideas on the fundamental problems

H

of church-state relationship in a coherent form. The cast of his mind was inimical to abstract ideas and general principles. His writings are, with few exceptions, directed immediately to current questions; he discussed what lay before his eyes; and he was stimulated by immediate circumstances rather than by broad considerations of policy. His comments on the nature and authority of the church (to which reference has just been made) are not taken from any formal treatise on the subject, but from notes jotted down as the basis of a book which, in fact, he never completed. And even this abortive effort was not spontaneous— he was preparing it in reply to a once famous (or infamous) work by Matthew Tindal, *The rights of the Christian church asserted*, which, despite its title, attacked the very notion of the church as an independent society, and denied altogether that it could claim either divine origin or divine authority. It was the need to establish some basis from which to launch a counter-attack against Tindal that obliged Swift to formulate, however briefly, his views on the nature of the church and its relations with the state; and he confines himself to a series of detached statements, each of which is provoked by some assertion of Tindal's. But these statements, though they fall far short of a comprehensive treatment of the subject, are a sufficient indication of Swift's essential views; and it is in the light of these views that we must consider his political activities.

It is important to remember that when Swift wrote to the 'church' we may normally assume that he was thinking of the Church of England, in which term he also comprehended the Church of Ireland. He was, of course, aware that the Christian religion extended beyond these islands; but it was natural to him (as has been said) to concentrate on the immediate circumstances, and it was the position of the Church of England rather than the Church Universal that lay before his eyes. It might seem, at first sight, that his views, as here described, would accord so ill with the actual condition of the Church of England in his day that he should have been driven to take up a revolutionary position. But though Swift was a High Churchman, he was not what his contemporaries would have called a 'high-flyer'. In practice, he was more influenced by the actual power of the state to control the church than by the divine right of the church to govern itself. After all, he was fighting a defensive battle: the Church of

England was under attack, and the best line of defence was to try to hold things as they were, lest worse befall. Any defiance of the civil power in the interests of ecclesiastical independence was unlikely to succeed, was certain to alienate allies, and would probably bring reinforcements to the enemy. It was much better to make sure, as far as possible, that the civil power was in the hands of the church's friends, and to guard against the danger that it should fall into the hands of her foes.

It was partly because he took this line that so much of Swift's activity in defence of the church was inextricably bound up with secular politics. But this is not the whole story. Swift did not take to politics simply in order to defend the Church of England—he was not one of those 'priests in politics' who have turned politicians in order to promote a pre-determined ecclesiastical programme. It would be nearer the truth to say that he found himself in politics, and was then obliged by conscience to defend the church. It is reasonable to say 'found himself in politics', for Swift's entry into political life was almost accidental. His first political pamphlet, *A discourse of the dissensions of Athens and Rome*, published in 1701, is a kind of academic exercise in defence of the whigs, and was written at the suggestion of his patron, Lord Berkeley. But it came at a time when the whig leaders felt the need of public support; they recognized that the author was an ally worth having; and though they did little or nothing for him, they entertained him with hopes. The publication of *A tale of a tub* in 1704 firmly established Swift's reputation as a writer; and, in an age when literature and politics were so closely intermingled, this added considerably to his political importance. Swift, who was never disposed to underrate his claims, could now feel that the whigs owed him something; and he increasingly resented their failure to secure his preferment. He had another source of uneasiness in the whig alliance with the dissenters, and the consequent danger (as Swift saw it) to the Church of England. It is tempting, at first sight, to assume that the two grievances went hand in hand; and to suppose that if the whigs had only made Swift a dean or bishop he would have left them free to treat the dissenters as liberally as they chose. But the evidence of chronology (apart from any other consideration) makes this interpretation very difficult to sustain.

We can see from Swift's letters to his friends that by 1707, at the latest, he had become seriously alarmed at the whigs' attitude to the church. They were still in office, he was still on friendly terms with their leaders, and it was to them that he must look for any promotion. But he felt that he must make his position clear: he would not continue to support them unless he was satisfied that their policy in ecclesiastical matters was one that he could approve. In three pamphlets written in 1708 he set out his point of view. *The sentiments of a Church of England man* deals, in fairly general terms, with the position and claims of the Church of England. The language is restrained and unprovocative; Swift is not openly challenging his friends to quarrel with him; but he does not equivocate on the main issue—his conviction that the well-being of the church is bound up with the maintenance of its privileges. The second pamphlet, *The argument against abolishing Christianity*, is a satirical attack on the free-thinkers; and though this did not involve a direct attack on the whigs, its whole attitude was unsympathetic to the known, or suspected, outlook of many of their leaders. They certainly did not relish Swift's line of argument; and he must have known, when he published it, the kind of reception they would give it.

The third pamphlet, written in 1708 (though not published until the following year), was the *Letter concerning the sacramental test*. This is in a somewhat different category from the others, for it was a direct and open attack on a policy that the ministry was known to favour: the relief of protestant dissenters in Ireland from the incidence of the sacramental test imposed in 1704. *The sentiments of a Church of England man* and the *Argument against abolishing Christianity*, though unpalatable to the whigs and likely enough to damage Swift's prospects with them, did not make a breach inevitable. The *Letter concerning the sacramental test* was a clear defiance; after this he could hope for nothing from a whig ministry.

It would be rash to assert that in thus publishing his position to the world Swift was wholly uninfluenced by any consideration other than the safety of the Church of England. He was disappointed at the failure of the ministry to extend Queen Anne's Bounty to the Irish clergy; he was disappointed, in a more personal way, at being passed over for the bishopric of Waterford. But the views he expressed in these pamphlets are the views that he consistently held, and not infrequently made public, throughout his career. There is nothing in his character or conduct at any point to suggest that he would have held back if the whigs had treated him more generously; and he had certainly no prospect of immediate advantage from alienating them in 1708-9: even if, as is possible, he was already edging towards an alliance with the tories, the three pamphlets we have been considering were not particularly adapted to assist him. Whatever mixture of motives Swift may have had, the determining factor was his resolution to speak out on behalf of the church, without regard to the effect on his own prospects.

We can deduce something of Swift's attitude from the circumstances surrounding another pamphlet that he wrote about this time, but did not publish. This was the *Story of the injured lady*, his first pamphlet on Irish affairs, composed in 1707. In it we can find, under a rather elaborate allegory, almost all the ideas on Anglo-Irish relations that he was later to put forward more clearly and more vigorously—Ireland's claim to equality with England, the rights of the Irish parliament, condemnation of the appointment of Englishmen to lucrative posts in Ireland and of the restraints placed upon Irish trade, the suggestion that Ireland's best retaliation would be to stop buying English goods and to live on her own resources. Everything, in fact, that is characteristic of Swift's championship of Ireland against England is already present, in 1707, in the *Story of the injured lady*. But the pamphlet remained unpublished until after Swift's death; and it was not until 1720 that he began to propagate, by degrees, the ideas that he had worked out almost half a generation earlier.

Why this delay? We may assume, in the first place, that he wrote the pamphlet because he was living in Ireland at the time and could not help being impressed by the poverty of the country. It was natural to him to set down his ideas on paper, and natural also to condemn what he regarded as injustice. But though he was living in Ireland, his hopes were still set on a career in England; and to appear as the champion of Irish rights could do him nothing but disservice with any English party. He certainly had no sense of obligation to Ireland or Irishmen which might counter his natural self-interest; so he laid the pamphlet aside, and left the woes of Ireland to look after themselves until permanent exile once more brought them before his eyes, and until the disappointment of his ambitions left him nothing to hope or to fear from English politicians.

Here, then, we have an illuminating contrast between Swift's attitude to Ireland and his attitude to the church. He did not feel committed to Ireland; and though he saw the injustice under which she suffered, he was prepared to keep quiet about it rather than risk offending those to whom he must look for advancement. But he did feel committed to the church, and was ready to defend her interests at any cost to himself.

Accepting the view that Swift's conduct in 1708 and 1709 was governed by his regard for the welfare of the church, can we go further and say that the same motive determined his course of action in 1710? It might seem logical to argue that since he had broken with the whigs because he disapproved of their ecclesiastical policy, he joined the tories because he found theirs satisfactory. Something might be said in support of this interpretation. The tories were generally regarded as the 'church party': they certainly showed themselves more co-operative than the whigs on the question of Queen Anne's Bounty, which was now extended to the Irish clergy, and in other respects also (e.g. in its attitude to the dissenters) the new ministry was much more to Swift's liking than the old. But to read the situation thus is to over-simplify it, for it involves the omission of one very important factor—Swift's personal ambition. His actual entry into politics had been almost accidental; but it accorded well with his earlier hopes, and offered an outlet for the powers of which he was conscious. He enjoyed the company of the great; he enjoyed the sense of being at the centre of things, of being among those by whom important decisions were made and of having a share in the making of those decisions. He threw in his lot with the tories, not because he could thus forward the interests of the church, but because the tories showed that they valued his alliance—Harley, in particular, realized how useful Swift could be—and because they were ready to treat him as he felt he should be treated, as the equal of the best man among them. It is only fair to Swift to say that he used his influence, as occasion offered, in the interests of the church, and that he would not have continued to serve the tories if their policy had run counter to that interest. But these are, on the whole, negative considerations; they explain why Swift remained with the tories (or, rather, why he did not leave them, as he had left the whigs); but they do not explain why he had joined them so promptly on their accession to power. That action arose primarily, if not entirely, from his own desire for position and influence.

The events of the years 1708–10 illustrate more clearly than those of any other period in Swift's life the true character of his position as 'a priest in politics'. He was not the dedicated cleric for whom political life is simply the means of advancing some ecclesiastical interest. He is not, at the other extreme, the politician who is only a cleric, as it were, by accident, and whose profession has the same sort of bearing on his political character as, for example, the law or the army might have on the barrister or the soldier who took to politics. There is a dualism in Swift's position, which draws something from both these extremes, but leaves him different from either. He accepted a political career, when the opportunity offered, and pursued it with zest, partly because he enjoyed the excitement, the bustle, the influence that it brought, but mainly as a means of establishing his position. He wanted, above everything else in this world, to be a great man among great men, to be treated like a lord, not like a provincial parson or a mere party pamphleteer. But this is only one aspect of the picture. He could not shed, he never thought of shedding, the clerical character that he had voluntarily assumed. And he accepted without reservation the duty that that character imposed, the duty of serving the interests of the church. It might be said, perhaps, that the influence of this duty upon his politics was almost wholly negative, that he was alert to defend the church when he thought her in danger, but that in the period of his greatest influence he had no scheme of ecclesiastical reform or improvement to put forward. This is substantially true, though it does not necessarily indicate any indifference on Swift's part: according to his view of church-state relations it was the duty of the civil power to protect the church, not to legislate for it. But the negative character of Swift's policy probably lies deeper, in a pessimism (which grew stronger as the years passed) about the future of the church and of Christianity itself. It is difficult to escape the impression, as one goes through his correspondence, that he saw his battle for the rights of the church as a rearguard action, which must, indeed, be fought to the end, but of which the end was hardly in doubt.

Swift's junction with the tories in 1710 was followed by a few years of activity and influence in affairs of state. When we speak of him as a 'priest in politics' it is to this period that our thoughts most readily turn. But we must remember that for the greater part of his political career he might more aptly be described as a 'priest out of politics'. If there is any paradox here, it is easily resolved. From around 1700 until 1714 Swift was in contact, more or less closely from time to time, with those in power; and even when his influence was at its lowest he could still hope that some change in the situation would bring him forward. But with 1714 all this comes abruptly to an end. Thenceforward, his exclusion from the ministerial circle was as complete and final as his exile to Ireland. He could, and did, still take an interest in political questions; but he could no longer exercise direct personal influence on the men who made and executed government policy. We may say that he remained a 'political priest'; but he was, in a very important sense, outside politics.

Though there is this sharp contrast between the period preceding 1714 and the period following, there is a remarkable element of continuity in Swift's political attitudes. He still enjoyed the exercise of power, whether in the petty politics of the chapter-house and the liberties of his cathedral, or in his control of the Dublin mob. And we may say, without being oversubtle, that in his championship of Irish rights he was seeking power vicariously. Forced into exile, branded as an Irishman, he was determined that the country in which he was obliged to live should enjoy the liberties to which he felt himself entitled. 'Am I a free man in England, and do I become a slave in six hours by crossing the channel?'—the use of the first person singular is more than a mere device of rhetoric: Swift felt every restraint on Ireland as if it were a personal insult; or, perhaps we should say, he felt it because to him it *was* a personal insult.

As before 1714, so afterwards, Swift's desire for power was qualified by his sense of duty to the church. The conflict between these two motives of his political life was less strongly marked in the latter period than in the former—he could no longer hope for direct influence within the ministry, nor expect any professional advancement; but the conflict was still there. If his campaign for the improvement of the Irish economy and the establishment of Irish rights was to have any prospect of success it must first secure widespread support in Ireland itself, there must be mutual confidence and unity of purpose at least within the politically-active section of the population, which meant, in effect, the protestant population. But even to secure this end Swift would not abate one jot of the church's claims. No man was more active than he in asserting the rights of the Irish parliament against England; but when the house of commons dared to lay a finger on the 'sacred tenth', no consideration of political expediency could hold Swift back. The language of his private letters is strong enough; but the language in which he published his indignation to the world is too vividly picturesque for quotation.

The same refusal to sacrifice the church for the sake of political unity, however desirable, appears in Swift's attitude to the protestant dissenters. The most famous of the *Drapier's letters* was addressed to 'the whole people of Ireland', and one might not unreasonably suppose this term to include the dissenters. But when the dissenters, still seeking relief from the sacramental test, issued an address to the members of the established church in which they referred to them as 'brother protestants and fellow Christians', Swift was roused to contemptuous anger. He was not going to be called 'brother' by any presbyterian. In a set of those rattling tetrameter verses that he handled so well he strung together a series of incongruous uses of the word 'brother' to disguise fundamental differences between the true and the false. And he took occasion, by the way, to characterize two of the best-known lawyers of the time:

> So, at the bar, the booby Bettesworth,
> Though half-a-crown o'er pays his sweat's worth,
> Knowing in law nor text nor margent,
> Calls Singleton his 'Brother Serjeant'.

Swift was not, of course, alone in resisting the claims of the dissenters. The great majority of the Irish house of commons showed itself so hostile that the government dared not even bring the question forward in any formal way. But, after all, Swift must be credited with more political insight than the average M.P. He, if any man, was capable of understanding that the cause of Ireland would be immensely strengthened by united protestant action. It is worth remembering that commercial freedom and constitutional rights were not obtained until Anglicans and presbyterians stood shoulder to shoulder in the Volunteers; and it is significant that the relief of the dissenters from the sacramental test, when it came in 1780, was regarded by Lord North's ministry as a concession to Irish national feeling. But, for Swift, no national advantage was worth the sacrifice of the church's safety.

It remains only to ask why Swift should have resisted so fiercely claims that seem to most of us so reasonable, claims, moreover, that would appear to follow naturally from his own famous dictum: 'Government without the consent of the governed is the very definition of slavery'. Some would find the answer in a narrow-minded sectarianism; some say that he had learned to hate the presbyterians during his brief residence in County Antrim. But the truth is that Swift's reluctance to admit dissenters to any share of poltical power flows directly from his views on the church and on its relations with the state. He quite sincerely regarded the Church of England, in its policy and doctrine (though not, of course, in its actual operation) as a model of apostolic purity. But this church had a dual existence. It was a divinely-instituted society, deriving its authority from Christ. It was also (as a result of an assumed contract) the official expression of the national religion; in this latter capacity it was subject to the supreme power of the state. In the *Argument against abolishing Christianity* Swift discussed whether or not the abolition of Christianity would affect the position of the established church. In the first place, of course, this is just another satirical stroke in his distinction between nominal and real Christianity. But we may take it also as hinting at a danger, of which Swift was always conscious, that the supreme power might take over the whole framework of the national church and transfer it to some form of Christianity other than the existing Church of England. In Swift's view, such action would be not only a breach of contract but contrary to the laws of God. But this did not make it impossible; and the only way to guard against it was to make sure that the supreme power (which for Swift was the legislature) remained safely in the hands of those who supported the existing constitution of the church. He was convinced that the dissenters, if they once acquired political influence, were bound by their own principles and professions to use it for the very purpose he most dreaded, the destruction of that church which he regarded 'as the most perfect of all others in discipline and doctrine', the Church of England.

Seven

Anglo-Irish Constitutional Relations in the Later Eighteenth Century

FEW periods of Irish history have been more extensively written about than the later eighteenth century: a mere list of books and papers dealing with the Volunteer movement, 'Grattan's parliament', the insurrection of 1798 and the legislative union of 1800 would make up a moderate-sized volume. Most of these writings are concerned, directly or indirectly, with the constitutional relationship between Ireland and Great Britain. Indeed, it might be said that this relationship is the basic theme in the Irish history of the period, even for social and economic historians; and the pattern is so well-established that it may well seem rash to assume that it can be substantially modified, or even made significantly clearer, except, perhaps, by the production of new and hitherto unsuspected evidence. Yet there is something to be said for looking again at the whole subject on the basis of our existing knowledge; not simply, as Irish historians are inclined to do, from the standpoint of Ireland, nor yet as if events in Ireland were a mere appendage to British history, but rather, as Professor Butterfield has done for one brief period in his *George III, Lord North and the people*, to consider Anglo-Irish constitutional relations during the late eighteenth century as part of the general political history of the British Isles.

Lest anyone should suppose that there is here a blind or slovenly confusion between the terms 'constitutional' and 'political', it should be made clear at the outset that the interchange is deliberate. Whether any valid distinction can be maintained between 'constitutional history' and 'political history' is not here in question; but it is essential to realize that there can be no fruitful discussion of Anglo-Irish constitutional relations, at least during this period, unless one takes into account not only legal rights and

123

formal procedures, but also the character, composition and connexions of political groups in both kingdoms. That it was the
action of such groups that brought about a formal change in
the constitutional relationship of Ireland to Great Britain in 1782
is self-evident; it is perhaps less obvious, but certainly not less
important, that the actual working out of the relationship, both
before and after the formal change had been made, was determined by the political situation.

The most significant of the changes made in 1782 were the repeal of the declaratory act of 1720 (the 'sixth of George I') and the
modification of Poynings' law; and the truth of what has been said
about the influence of the political situation is borne out by an
examination of these changes. The power to legislate for Ireland,
as asserted by the British parliament in the declaratory act, was not
formally limited in any way; but it was, in practice, very cautiously
used. There was never any question of taxing Ireland by British
legislation; and even in less vital matters ministers were very unwilling to stir up trouble by using the authority of a British statute
to override the will of the Irish parliament. In the early 1730s, for
example, when they found their intention of repealing the sacramental test, so far as it affected protestant dissenters, blocked by
the opposition of the house of commons, they never seriously
considered getting round the difficulty by using the legislative
authority of the British parliament.[1] British legislation for Ireland
between 1720 and 1782 was, in fact, very largely economic or
administrative, the great bulk of it applying to the whole British
Isles or the whole empire; and much of it was of such a character that if Ireland had been excluded, the Irish parliament would
have had to pass similar legislation itself.

Irish opinion came to regard the declaratory act as a grievance,
not because Ireland was being continually harassed by fresh
British legislation, but partly because some British acts, very few
in number, did seriously limit the freedom of Irish trade, and
partly because the very fact that the British parliament could
legislate for Ireland at all was a galling reminder of Ireland's
inferior status. The two grievances were, so to speak, complemen-
tary. Had there been no economic oppression, it would have been
difficult to raise a national clamour against a legislative power
that was otherwise beneficial, or at least harmless, in its effects.
The national clamour, once raised, could not be stilled by a mere

removal of the oppression; and Irish pride could not be satisfied without the repeal of the declaratory act in 1782, and the passage of the renunciation act in the following year.

But though the passage of these measures marked a formal change in Anglo-Irish constitutional relationship, a practical change, due to the pressure of political circumstances, can be detected some years earlier. The fear of arousing parliamentary opposition in Ireland by too open use of British legislative power had become much stronger, and between 1775 and 1782 special British legislation for Ireland was confined almost entirely to measures either repealing restrictive statutes, about which Ireland had complained, or conferring positive benefits.[2] The circumstances that had produced this nervous regard for Irish opinion remained substantially unchanged after 1782; and it seems reasonable to suppose that even if the declaratory act had remained in force the British parliament would have refrained from legislating for Ireland in defiance of the Irish house of commons. The right of legislation asserted in the declaratory act had been exercised before the act was passed, and might have fallen into practical disuse even though the act had remained unrepealed.

A study of the operation of Poynings' law before and after 1782 suggests a conclusion of the same general character. By the middle of the eighteenth century the role of the Irish council in relation to Poynings' law seems to have become little more than formal: except in preparation for a new parliament, it rarely, if ever, drew up bills in advance; and it seems practically to have abandoned its right to suppress or modify heads of bills presented to it by either house of parliament.[3] In forwarding bills to the British council the lord lieutenant frequently expressed views about the proposed measures; but it was in England, not in Ireland, that their fate was decided.

At the beginning of each parliamentary session in Ireland the British council appointed a committee[4]

> to consider the bills which shall be transmitted from Ireland, during the present session of parliament there, together with the reports to be made thereupon by his majesty's attorney and solicitor general, and all petitions relating thereto; and their lordships are from time to time to report to his majesty at this board what alterations and amendments they conceive proper to be made to such bills.

Generally speaking, down to 1782, the law officers simply recommended that a measure be accepted, amended, or 'respited'; and the available evidence suggests that such recommendations were usually accepted by the committee (and, in turn, by the council) as a matter of course. When, as occasionally happened, the law officers expressed doubts, but made no firm recommendation, the committee presumably made up its mind for itself.[5] The total number of 'respited' bills seems to have been relatively small; but it included many that were popular in Ireland, and whose suppression was a source of grievance. The proportion of bills amended was much higher; and though the amendments often affected the form rather than the substance (and were, indeed, sometimes necessary to correct faulty drafting), the practice was commonly regarded in Ireland as a constitutional grievance. This was particularly so with regard to money bills; and more than once the Irish commons rejected such bills simply on the ground that they had been altered in England.[6] But the council insisted on its rights; and even when money bills transmitted from Ireland were in all respects satisfactory, it was the custom to make 'one or two literal amendments . . . solely for preserving the right of amending those bills'.[7] In the late 1770s, when the ministry was anxious not to exacerbate Irish feeling, some care seems to have been taken to keep alterations to a minimum: in December 1779, for example, Bathurst (lord president of the council), in returning a group of bills to Ireland, drew Buckinghamshire's attention to the fact that they were returned unaltered 'which I hope will be agreeable'; and when, a year later, it was thought necessary to alter a bill relating to the sugar trade, he wrote an almost apologetic note of explanation.[8]

The modification of Poynings' law in 1782 affected formal procedure in England in one way only. Since a bill was no longer liable to be amended, there was no need to delay engrossment until it had passed the council; as soon as it had done so the great seal of England could be affixed to the engrossed copy sent over from Ireland, which could then be returned at once. This meant a great speeding up of the process: on at least one occasion, a bill reached London in the morning, and was sent off on its return journey the same evening.[9]

In other respects, things went on as before: there was still a committee for Irish bills, which reported to the council after consultation with the law officers of the crown.[10] But the process soon tended to become formalized. The reports of the law officers seldom do more than list the bills they have considered, and certify that in their opinion they 'ought to receive his majesty's assent and pass into laws'.[11] On the very rare occasions on which they offer any comment, their recommendations are cautiously worded. On 30th April 1784, for example, they presented a long report on Foster's press law, and concluded

> That it not being competent for us to make any alterations in the bill, we have thought it necessary in such a case to state its effects; and that it belongs to your lordships to determine whether the circumstances which induced the legislature of Ireland to pass this bill make it proper that it should receive his majesty's royal assent, and pass into a law.[12]

But on this and on all similar occasions the council was very reluctant to exercise its power of veto; and though bills were sometimes held up for further discussion, it would seem that during the whole period down to the union all, with a few unimportant exceptions,[13] eventually were returned to Ireland.

During the debate on Poynings' law in the Irish house of commons, in June 1782,[14] the advocates of an explicit repeal objected strongly to leaving the power of suppression in the hands of the British council; and even those who supported Yelverton spoke as if they expected this power to be used. On the British side, the maintenance of Poynings' law, in some form, was certainly regarded as a necessary safeguard for the constitutional connection between the kingdoms.[15] But in spite of these fears and expectations, Yelverton's act proved to be, in practice, virtually the equivalent of repeal; for the British ministers were unwilling to use the powers they had been so anxious to retain. And the reason for their unwillingness is to be found mainly in the fact that they could not afford to risk arousing Irish feeling against them: after the passage of Yelverton's act, as before, political circumstances in the two kingdoms modified in practice the formal constitutional relations between them.

The conclusion to be drawn from these comments on the declaratory act and Poynings' law is certainly not that the changes made in 1782 were unimportant; it is rather that those changes must be seen as part of a process. The constitutional relationship between

Ireland and Great Britain changed considerably during the later eighteenth century; but the change did not begin and end in 1782. There was, in fact, a period of constitutional development, which began before 1782, and continued afterwards. It is to the background and character of this development that we must now turn our attention.

From the end of Queen Anne's reign until the 1770s Ireland was almost outside the range of British politics. Irish appointments might be a matter of bargaining or dispute between rival parties and factions; Irish politicians might sometimes be able to use their English connexions to secure or retain office; at long intervals some outburst of political excitement in Dublin might arouse a passing anxiety in London. But, in general, the government of Ireland was regarded as a matter of routine, to be conducted on well-understood principles, about which British statesmen, however deeply divided on other subjects, were in agreement; no ministry felt it necessary to have an 'Irish policy'; and the viceroyalty did not normally change hands with a change of ministers in England. The ending of this state of affairs in the 1770s formed an essential background to the constitutional developments of the later eighteenth century.

The way for the change was prepared by the growth of the patriot movement in Ireland and by the sharpening of the party conflict at Westminster; the constitutional struggle between Great Britain and her American colonies contributed to both developments, and the outbreak of the American war, in April 1775, marked a critical turning-point. In any circumstances the war would have made the state of Ireland a matter of greater concern to the ministry, if only because the restriction of colonial trade enhanced the importance of the Irish market for British goods. But Lord North had more to think about than this; for there was a danger that unless Irish opinion could be conciliated a new America might arise just across the channel. North thus found himself faced with the difficult task of working out an Irish policy. Nor was he left in peace to adapt the established principles of Irish government to meet new conditions; for the opposition leaders at Westminster, eager to embarrass him by every possible means, took up the patriot cause, and came forward with an Irish policy of their own. Though constitutional issues were, to begin with, only indirectly involved, they could not long be ignored;

and the whole question of Anglo-Irish relations became a matter of political dispute in Great Britain.

The British opposition was certainly not moved by any altruistic concern for Irish welfare. Even Burke always considered the interests of Ireland as of subordinate importance, and a few years earlier had lent his support to the great whig landlords who had engineered the defeat of the proposal to tax absentees. But if there is some truth in the charge that Rockingham and Shelburne, Richmond and Fox, acted selfishly, even irresponsibly, in bringing Ireland into British party politics, it must be admitted that the circumstances provide some justification for their conduct. The great issue was the American war. The ministry was desperately anxious to justify its policy in the eyes of the world, the opposition no less anxious to show that that policy was foolish, immoral and unpopular. Both sides therefore attached great importance to expressions of public opinion; and even Irish opinion, usually little attended to in England, acquired a new significance. When the Irish parliament met in October 1775 it was the first business of the viceroy, Harcourt, to secure from the house of commons a firm declaration of support for the war. Though he succeeded in doing so, an opposition amendment calling for conciliation was defeated only after a violent debate. He followed up his success by winning parliamentary approval for the withdrawal of troops; but once again the debate revealed a strong body of opinion hostile to the war. It was natural enough that the British whigs should try to weaken the ministry by encouraging this opposition in Dublin and by taking up its cause at Westminster.

The patriots were thus convinced that a change of political fortune in England would give their allies control of the Castle, and open the way for the fulfilment of all their own hopes. The real attitude of the whigs to Anglo-Irish relations was not, in fact, very different from North's; but having chosen a line of conduct they could not abandon it, and when the time came they found themselves committed to the whole patriot programme. The alliance thus established between whigs and patriots was to survive, in some form, until the end of the century; and the existence of this alliance, however tenuous it might at times appear, exercised an almost continuous influence over the constitutional relations between the two kingdoms.

The nature and effect of this alliance can be clearly seen in the

I

events of March and April 1782. With the fall of North's ministry there was an immediate change in the viceroyalty: Carlisle was recalled with almost indecent haste, and Portland was appointed to succeed him. This marked such a sharp contrast with previous practice that it must be regarded as significant, despite the fact that in other branches of government also the changes accompanying the accession to power of the Rockingham whigs were more extensive than had been customary on similar occasions in the past. What was much more significant, however, was the reaction of Irish opinion. The speech in which Grattan moved his address to the crown (his famous 'Declaration of independence') on 16th April was not an appeal for justice, it was not much concerned with explaining or defending the rights of Ireland; it was a hymn of triumph over a victory already won. But in point of fact the only victory already won was that of the British whigs; and there could be no more striking proof of the intermingling of British and Irish politics at this point than Grattan's assumption, fully justified in the sequel, that this involved a victory for the patriots also.

The link between party politics in Ireland and in Great Britain created a constitutional problem to which historians have rarely paid much attention, and of which contemporaries, though they were aware of its existence, did not grasp the full implications. The problem was practical rather than theoretical, and it cannot be simply stated in a general form, but in essence it came to this: since, as now seemed to be the case, a change of administration in England was to be followed by a change of administration in Ireland, it was almost inevitable that opposition leaders in the two countries would work together; in these circumstances, and given the co-existence of two independent legislatures, how was the continuity of British government in Ireland to be maintained, and the permanent connexions between Great Britain and Ireland guaranteed?

British statesmen may not have seen the problem in precisely these terms; but they could not fail to recognize that the old system of relationship, based on the subordination of Ireland, had finally come to an end; and that some other system must be put in its place, though their notions of what the new system was to be were narrowly, or at least inadequately, conceived. Shelburne and Portland at first hoped to solve the problem by persuading the

Irish to leave the British parliament 'a superintending power . . . for all purposes of common concern whether in matters of state or general commerce';[16] and when this proved impossible they confined themselves, for the time being, to the negative task of resisting 'any further attempts which may *possibly* be made to encroach upon the British government, or his majesty's known prerogative'.[17]

Two years later, the problem was still unsolved. 'We are all sensible', wrote Pitt to Rutland, in July 1784,[18]

> of the necessity of forming upon due deliberation some systematic line of conduct, which, when thoroughly weighed, must be steadily adhered to, as the only chance of extricating the interests of this country in Ireland from the delicate situation in which they are placed . . .'

But Pitt saw the problem of Anglo-Irish relations mainly in economic terms:[19]

> In the relation of Great Britain [with Ireland] there can subsist but two possible principles of connection. The one, that which is exploded, of total subordination in Ireland, and of restrictions on her commerce for the benefit of this country, which was by this means enabled to bear the whole burden of the empire; the other is, what is now proposed to be confirmed and completed, that of an equal participation of all commercial advantages, and some proportion of the charge of protecting the general interest. If Ireland is at all connected with this country, and to remain a member of the empire, she must make her option between these two principles, and she has wisely and justly made it for the latter.

The problem, however, was not fundamentally an economic one; and even if Pitt's scheme had been accepted, the constitutional difficulty would have remained. It might, indeed, have become more serious: for while Pitt was determined to get a financial contribution from Ireland, he was equally determined that the Irish parliament should have no effective check on its expenditure, lest this might 'let them into a control on the executive government of the empire which must *completely* reside here'.[20]

Shelburne and Portland sought to base a new system on constitutional safeguards, Pitt on a commercial treaty. But, at bottom, the maintenance of harmonious relations between the two kingdoms depended on the ability of the lord lieutenant to manage

parliament. Thomas Pelham saw that this was so; and he saw also
that party alignments were significant. But his account of the
position in 1783 was, in one important respect, strangely out of
date:

> In my opinion there are two parties in this country, as well as in
> England, but their principle is very different, their objects are
> different, and their institution dissimilar. In England, the object
> is to bring themselves and friends into power under some par-
> ticular minister; in Ireland, no exertions can be attended with
> such consequences. Here, I apprehend it may be fairly said, that
> the supporters of administration are the friends to English
> government; opposition consists of men unfriendly to England,
> county members under the influence of their electors, and a few
> disappointed individuals, who are hostile to the reigning lord
> lieutenant.[21]

What Pelham overlooked was that now an Irish opposition
could hope to come into office; not, indeed, simply by winning a
parliamentary majority, but by alliance with a British party. How
else had so many of the patriot leaders gained position and power
in 1782 and 1783? Pelham was, perhaps, blinded by prejudice. As
an Englishman, he felt that all parties should combine to keep
Ireland in its place: 'I am clear that it is the interest of every party
in England to encourage the supporters of English government in
Ireland; very improper means have been used under different
administrations to secure this point, but the principle should
never be abandoned'.[22] As an English whig, he despised those who
passed under that denomination in Ireland.[23] But he could not
alter the facts. There were Irish whigs, however despicable; they
looked for guidance and support to their allies in England; and
some at least of the latter were ready to use their influence in Ireland for party ends.

The conduct of Portland, under whose aegis he had taken office
as chief secretary, forms a curious commentary on Pelham's view
of Irish politics. Portland had used his brief viceroyalty to such
effect that he could claim, in 1783, the allegiance of one-sixth of
the house of commons—'those whom I have the vanity to call my
friends . . . and whom I consider collectively as the nest-egg of a
real whig party'. It was on these members that he urged Northington, the lord lieutenant, to place his main reliance;[24] and when
Northington, finding that their strength was insufficient, brought

about a 'concurrence' between them and the former supporters of
Carlisle's administration,[25] Portland complained that the affair
had been mismanaged, and raised difficulties about the proposed
new appointments. Very significantly, he regarded the conjunction
of forces in Ireland as parallel with that which had previously
taken place in England: 'In the formation of the coalition on this
side of the water . . . excepting the office held by Lord North . . .
every efficient office was reserved for our own friends. . . . If,
therefore, in submitting to the necessity of a coalition in Ireland
as well as here, the same line had been adhered to, I should not
have had occasion to give you this trouble. . . .'[26] It is, perhaps,
hardly surprising, though it is sharply at variance with the principle laid down by Pelham, that when the Fox-North coalition fell,
and the government of Ireland passed from Northington to Rutland, the new viceroy found in 'the duke of Portland's faction' a
serious threat to his control of the house of commons.[27]

In these circumstances, it was no longer possible, as in earlier
days, to divide Irish politicians simply into the friends and
enemies of 'English connection', for 'English connection' itself
was no longer a simple concept: the very fact that the viceroyalty
was now liable to change with every change of ministry under-
mined both the unity and the continuity of British policy in Ireland. But though political leaders on both sides of the channel
were ready to draw party advantage from this new state of affairs,
it is doubtful if they really understood it. Their language, and
their actions, certainly suggest some confusion of thought. Portland, though he wanted to make Ireland a field for whig politics,
recommended the embryonic Irish whigs to Northington as 'the
real friends of English government';[28] yet in the previous year he
had complained that Irish M.P.s commonly boasted of the support
they had given 'to *English government*', and that as a result 'the
distinction between administration and government is so totally
lost that it can hardly be said to exist'.[29] The letter in which he
urged Northington not to resign, on the fall of the coalition in
December 1783, shows something of the same confusion of attitudes; for on the one hand he argues that a change of viceroyalty at
this point would have a bad effect in Ireland; and on the other, he
asserts that the new ministry cannot last long, and suggests, by
implication, that as Northington's friends will soon be back in
power in England, he might as well retain office in the interval.[30]

Hillsborough's letter to Northington on the same occasion, also urging him not to resign, puts the relationship between the lord lieutenant and the ministry on a quite unrealistic basis: 'your connection with Lord North was not very binding, nor did I ever hear Mr. Fox had any particular claim to your attachment'; Northington (he goes on) had received his office 'from the king alone', and it might be considered improper for him to resign 'upon his majesty having obtained a victory'.[31] Pitt and Sydney, though on much more reasonable grounds, also wished to avoid, or at least to postpone, a change of viceroys, and were 'very anxious that the people of Ireland should be convinced of their disinclination to make any party distinctions'.[32] Northington's own estimate of the situation was much shrewder: he saw the need for close reciprocal confidence between the lord lieutenant and the cabinet; he was convinced that this confidence could not exist if he were to remain in office; and he insisted on resigning.[33] But Northington, clear-sighted enough on this point, does not seem to have realized the constitutional significance of his method of conducting the government. He put himself almost entirely in the hands of Grattan, with whom he regularly consulted about appointments and measures before they were submitted for the approval of the ministry in England.[34] Such a system, if long continued, might easily have led to the development of a separate administration, reflecting distinctively Irish interests and influences; and even during Northington's brief tenure of office there were occasions on which divergence of policy between Dublin and London strained the unity of the executive.[35]

The confusion revealed in the language and actions of so many contemporary statesmen arose not unnaturally from the twofold novelty of the situation that confronted them: they ignored or misunderstood the problems created by the linking up of party politics in the two kingdoms very largely because they were puzzled and disturbed by the formal change that had taken place in the constitutional relationship of one to the other. The change had been carried through hastily, under popular pressure, without preliminary negotiation; and no one knew exactly what it involved. Question after question occupied the attention of politicians and lawyers, and kept alive the feeling of uncertainty. What was now the position of the court of admiralty in Ireland?[36] Might not Ireland claim dominion over half the Irish Sea?[37] If the Irish post office was in future to be independent, how were the postal services of the two kingdoms to be linked together?[38] Since Irish bills were no longer liable to alteration in England, why should the attorney and solicitor-general continue to collect fees for scrutinizing private bills from Ireland?[39] How did legislative independence affect relations with foreign powers?[40]

It is not within the scope of this essay to treat any of these questions in detail; but during the 1780s they raised doubts, and opened possibilities of conflict, very disturbing to British statesmen whose main aim was to arrive at a final settlement with Ireland.[41] Small wonder, then, that the more subtle problems arising from the new relations in party politics were imperfectly considered. It might be argued that if these problems were as important as is here suggested, they would have forced themselves into notice, and demanded solution; but they were, in fact, obscured by the course of politics; the long continuance of Pitt's ministry re-established, though on a different and less secure basis, substantially the same relationship between British and Irish government as had existed earlier in the century; and it was easy to find Irish politicians who were willing, from interest or from principle, to maintain the old system.

But throughout this period the cross-channel link in party politics continued to exist; and it had a real, though fluctuating, influence on Anglo-Irish relations. Fox's boast, in May 1784, that he would 'make his harvest from Ireland',[42] though over-optimistic, was not an entirely empty one; he and his allies found in Irish affairs material for their attacks on Pitt in the British house of commons, and they used their influence in Ireland to undermine his government there. They were not wholly unsuccessful: the clamour in both kingdoms that killed the commercial propositions of 1785 was largely of their raising; and Rutland attributed the virtual defeat of the government in the Irish house of commons on 12th–13th August mainly to the defection of the Ponsonbys, under the influence of the 'Portland interest'.[43] As things turned out, this did the British opposition little good; but it was significant of the new state of affairs that Fox should have hoped, and Pitt feared,[44] that a failure in Ireland would affect the prospects of the ministry in England.

In the struggle over the commercial propositions Fox had appeared both as the defender of English economic interests against Irish competition and as the defender of Irish liberties against English oppression. Such an ambiguous rôle, easy for the opposition, was impossible for the government; but during the critical early years of his ministry Pitt was constantly obliged to consider the possible reaction of Irish as well as of English opinion to his policies. Rutland's success or failure in Ireland bore so directly on the stability of administration in England that nothing must be done to embarrass him. Fox and his allies took full advantage of this position, and lost no opportunity of bringing forward Irish issues. Under cover of the debates on the commercial treaty with France they tried to re-open discussion of the abortive propositions of 1785, with the double object of reviving English alarm and of creating Irish distrust of the ministry;[45] and they supported Ireland in the dispute with Portugal over the construction of the Methuen treaty.[46] There can be little doubt that the solicitude for Irish interests shown by Pitt and Eden in the French negotiations, and the persistent efforts of the ministry to secure an entry for Irish woollens into Portugal owed a good deal to the need for countering these tactics.[47] In February 1787 Rutland's correspondent, Daniel Pulteney, wrote of Sheridan and Flood as 'two self-appointed Irish ambassadors running a race for Irish popularity in an English house of commons';[48] it would hardly be an exaggeration to say that at this time such a race was, in fact, being run between government and opposition, but for them 'Irish popularity' was important as a means towards defending, or capturing, control of administration in England.

As Pitt's hold on office grew stronger the power of the opposition to damage him through Ireland declined, though the events of the regency crisis showed how easily it might be revived; and the continuing influence of party links between England and Ireland was revealed, in a rather different way, in the 'Fitzwilliam episode'. The fact that Pitt remained continuously in power for so long a period tended, as has been said already, to reproduce a system of Anglo-Irish constitutional relations not very dissimilar from that which had existed before 1782; but it tended also to identify that system with the maintenance of Pitt's ministry. Fitzgibbon and Beresford, the key figures in the Irish administration, were essentially Pitt's men. No influence save that of Pitt could have induced Fitzgibbon to accept the relief act of 1793; and two years later it was Pitt who vetoed the dismissal of Fitzgibbon and insisted on the reinstatement of Beresford. It would be misleading, however, to suggest that Fitzgibbon and Beresford thought of their co-operation with Pitt simply in party terms; for in view of the alliance between Irish and English whigs, and of their attitude to whig policy in Ireland, they were almost bound to regard loyalty to Pitt and loyalty to the British connexion as virtually the same thing. And whatever may be said about Pitt's conduct in 1794–5, his ultimate refusal to hand over Ireland completely to the Portlands was based on a determination to preserve the unity of the central executive. In the circumstances of the later 1790s it is hardly surprising that the final guarantee of British connexion and of executive unity should be sought in a legislative union, and that its great engineers should be Fitzgibbon and Pitt.

At first sight it might seem that the struggle over union should have been a sort of testing-point of the alliance between Irish and English whigs, revealing at once it strength, its character, and its influence on Anglo-Irish relations. But the struggle occurred at a time when men's minds were occupied by war abroad and the fear of revolution at home, and when the bulk of the opposition whigs had withdrawn in disgust from Westminster. The Irish opponents of union were thus left to fight alone, and without prospect of relief. Had there been any likelihood, or even possibility, of a change of administration in England the government's threat to make support for union an indispensable and universal test for every kind of office and favour would have lost much of its force, and many of those who sold out to Castlereagh, in the fear of being forced into perpetual opposition, would have stood their ground. It was Pitt's overwhelming strength at Westminster that enabled him to buy a majority in College Green.

Two points arise from this general survey. First, the constitutional relationship between Ireland and Great Britain during the later eighteenth century depended, in practice, not simply on formal enactments, but on the character of the whole political situation. This, it may be said, is no more than a truism, hardly worth stating, and certainly not requiring demonstration. But it is sometimes necessary, or at least useful, to remind ourselves of the obvious; and historians have laid such stress on the legislation of 1782 that one might almost be led to suppose that Ireland was governed, both before and after that date, by a strict interpretation of the letter of the law.

In the second place, the essential turning-point in Anglo-Irish relations came with the linking up of party politics in the two countries. The success of the patriots in 1782 was not due solely to their alliance with the British whigs; they themselves certainly believed that if there had been no change of ministry in England they could nevertheless have forced out of Lord North the concessions actually made by his successors. But in those circumstances the character of the 'constitution of 1782' would have been very different. No ministry headed by North, no viceroy nominated by him, could have inspired the degree of confidence accorded by the popular party in Ireland to the whigs. It was this confidence that preserved the stability of government during the critical period between the early summer of 1782 and the end of November 1783; without it, control of the house of commons by the Castle would have been almost impossible; the constitutional changes, instead of being accepted as a final settlement, would have been regarded as a basis for further demands; and Portland's prophecy, in May 1782, that in such circumstances 'the English government must be prepared to renounce all pretensions to respect or influence in this country'[49] might well have been fulfilled.

The co-operation between whigs and patriots enabled English influence to survive; but it survived on a basis of party alliance. A few days after his arrival in Dublin, Rutland had written hopefully of his desire 'to separate and keep away every mixture of English politics and party divisions from the conduct of affairs' in Ireland.[50] But the connexions established during the 1770s could not so quickly be broken; and men who believed that their prospects of keeping or gaining office might be directly affected by any change of administration in England were not easily persuaded that Irishmen had nothing to do with English party politics. Eighteen months later, Rutland had to admit that experience had taught him the necessity of distinguishing 'between those who support from principle and from attachment and those who, possessing great offices, wait only for a favourable opportunity to sacrifice their employers to the views and to the ambitions of the English faction'.[51] This continuing influence of 'English faction' came sharply to the surface in the crises of 1789 and 1794–5; its extent in more normal circumstances is indicated in some detail in the account of the house of commons in 1791, prepared by his political agent for the marquis of Abercorn.[52]

The conclusion to which these considerations bring us may be briefly stated. The character of Anglo-Irish constitutional relations during the later eighteenth century was modified by two related processes—the growth of Irish national sentiment, and a change in English attitudes to Irish affairs. These processes resulted in an intermingling of party politics in the two countries, with a consequent threat to the stability of government, and even to the survival of English influence, in Ireland. This threat, though temporarily averted by the long continuance of Pitt's ministry, never disappeared; and we may reasonably regard it as one of the main elements in the general confusion of Irish political life that led to the union of the two parliaments.

NOTES

1. J. C. Beckett, *Protestant dissent in Ireland, 1687–1780*, pp. 91–5.
2. See J. C. Beckett and A. G. Donaldson, 'The Irish parliament in the eighteenth century', in *Proceedings of the Belfast Natural History and Philosophical Society*, 2nd series, iv. 30–1.
3. But cf. Harcourt to Rochford, 24th Mar. 1774 (*Cal. H.O. Papers, 1773–5*, p. 198); *Irish parliamentary register*, i. 392.
4. P.R.O., P.C. 1. 15/50.
5. The committee of council for Irish bills sometimes took further advice on particular points: e.g. the tillage bill of 1766 was referred to the commissioners of customs (P.R.O., P.C. 1. 15/30); and in 1780 the question of the sugar duty was referred to the committee of trade (ibid., 1. 31/78).
6. E.g. in December 1773 (Harcourt to Rochford, 30th Dec. 1773, (*Cal. H.O. papers, 1773–5*, pp. 121–3), where reference is also made to earlier instances).
7. E.g. Granville to Bedford, 7th Dec. 1759; Granville to Halifax, 5th Dec. 1761; Winchilsea to Hertford, 10th Dec. 1765 (P.R.O., P.C. 1. 31/78).
8. Bathurst to Buckinghamshire, 16th Dec. 1779, 8th Aug. 1780 (ibid.); cf. Shelburne to Portland, 11th Apr. 1782 (P.R.O., H.O. 100/1, fo. 40).
9. Stormont to Northington, 12th Dec. 1783; Fawkener to Pelham, 20th Oct. 1796 (P.R.O., P.C. 1. 31/78).
10. [Nepean] to Orde, 18th Feb. 1786 (P.R.O., H.O. 100/18, ff. 64–7).
11. For the period Jan.–May 1784 there are formal reports of this kind on 61 bills; the only critical report during the period is that referred to in the text (P.R.O., P.C. 1. 16/12).
12. Ibid.
13. Lecky, *Ireland*, ii. 335–6. I have found only two bills that were

'respited' during the period, both in August 1785; one for granting bounties on gunpowder, one relating to the demise of the crown (P.R.O., P.C. 1. 31/78). But the subject requires further investigation.

14. *Irish parliamentary register*, i. 386 ff.

15. Shelburne to Portland, 29th Apr. 1782; Portland to Shelburne, 6th May 1782 (P.R.O., H.O. 100/1, ff. 144–144^V, 179–179^V).

16. Shelburne to Portland, 18th May 1782 (P.R.O., H.O. 100/1, fo. 218).

17. Same to same, 8th June 1782 (ibid., H.O. 100/2, ff. 7^V–8).

18. Pitt to Rutland, 28th July 1784 (*Correspondence of Pitt and Rutland, 1781–1787* (London, 1890), pp. 31–2).

19. Pitt to Rutland, 6th Jan. 1785 (ibid., p. 72).

20. Pitt to Orde, 12th Jan. 1784 (ibid., pp. 87–8).

21. [Pelham] to Portland [1783] (B.M., Add. MS. 33100, ff. 431–5).

22. Ibid.

23. 'I do not the less esteem the soundness of whig principles in England because that I despise the false profession of them in this country.' (Same to same, 24th Oct. 1783 (ibid., ff. 372–4).)

24. Portland to Northington, 18th Sept. 1783 (B.M., Add. MS. 38716, ff. 102^V, 104).

25. W. Eden to Northington, 19th Nov. [1783] (B.M., Add. MS. 33100, ff. 391–2).

26. Portland to Pelham, 27th Oct. 1783 (ibid., ff. 381–3).

27. Rutland to Sydney, 4th July 1785; Sydney to Rutland, 16th July 1785 (H.M.C., *Rutland*, iii. 221, 225). Cf. John Beresford to John Robinson, 11th Apr. 1784 [on the arrival of Rutland] 'Mr. Ponsonby waited for orders from the duke of Portland'. (W. Beresford (ed.), *Correspondence of the Rt Hon. John Beresford* (London, 1854), i. 253.)

28. Portland to Northington, 18th Sept. 1783 (B.M., Add. MS. 38716, fo. 102).

29. Portland to Shelburne, 24 Apr. 1782 (P.R.O., H.O. 100/1, fo. 135).

30. Same to Northington, 27th Dec. 1783 (B.M., Add. MS. 38716, ff. 148^V–9^V).

31. Hillsborough to Northington, 26th Dec. 1783 (B.M., Add. MS. 33100, ff. 496–7).

32. Pelham to Northington, [Dec. 1783] (ibid. ff. 527–30).

33. Northington to Sydney, 28th Dec. 1783 (P.R.O., H.O. 100/12, ff. 5–6). Portland, though he was now trying to induce Northington to remain in office, had a few months earlier laid even greater stress on the absolute necessity of confidence and co-operation between Dublin and London (Portland to Pelham, 2nd Aug. 1783 (B.M., Add. MS. 33100, ff. 237–8)).

34. Northington to Pelham, 10th Sept. 1783; same to Fox, 17th & 18th Nov. 1783 (B.M., Add. MS. 38716, ff. 88, 131^V–132); Northington to Pelham, 7th Sept. 1783; Pelham [?] to Windham, 14th Sept. 1783 (B.M., Add. MS. 33100, ff. 304–5, 318–19).

35. E.g. over the duty on sugar (Northington to Fox, 17th & 18th Nov. 1783 (B.M., Add. MS. 38716, ff. 129–129^V)).

36. Northington to North, 23rd Sept. 1783 (P.R.O., H.O. 100/10, fo. 106ᵛ).

37. Orde to Rutland, 9th June 1784 (H.M.C., *Rutland*, iii. 105).

38. Northington to North, 23rd Sept. 1783 (P.R.O., H.O. 100/10, f. 107ᵛ); North to Northington, 2nd Dec. 1783 (B.M., Add. MS. 38716, ff. 141–2).

39. Orde to Nepean, 9th Feb. 1786; Thurlow to [Sydney], 16th Feb. 1786; [Nepean] to Orde, 18th Feb. 1786 (P.R.O., H.O. 100/18, ff. 60–61, 432–33ᵛ, 64–7).

40. There was, for example, some demand for the appointment of Irish diplomatic representatives abroad (P.R.O., H.O. 100/5, ff. 55–9, H.O. 100/10, f. 104). In 1783 the question was raised whether the peace treaties should be laid before the Irish parliament. Northington to North, 29th Sept. 1783, North to Northington, 3rd Nov. 1783 (P.R.O., H.O. 100/10, ff. 128–9, 208).

41. Fox to Northington, 1st Nov. 1783 (B.M., Add. MS. 38716, ff. 136–136ᵛ); Pitt to Rutland, 4th Dec. 1784 (*Correspondence of Pitt and Rutland, 1781–1787*, p. 51).

42. Mornington to Rutland, 31st May 1784 (H.M.C., *Rutland*, iii. 99); Rutland to Pitt, 16th June 1784 (*Correspondence of Pitt and Rutland, 1781–1787*, p. 22).

43. Rutland to Pitt, 4th July 1785; same to same, 17th Aug. 1785 (ibid., pp. 108–9, 122–3).

44. Pitt to Rutland, 21st May 1785 (ibid., pp. 104–7).

45. Daniel Pulteney to Rutland, 20th Feb. 1787 (H.M.C., *Rutland*, iii, 373).

46. Same to same, 10th Feb. 1787 (ibid., iii. 371).

47. Rutland to Sydney, 11th Mar., 4th Nov. 1786 (P.R.O., H.O. 100/18, ff. 131–5, 403). Eden to Beresford, 20th Apr., 15th Sept., 3rd Oct. 1786 (*Correspondence of J. Beresford*, i. 303, 312, 313).

48. Daniel Pulteney to Rutland, 22nd Feb. 1787 (H.M.C., *Rutland*, iii. 374). Mr. M. J. Barnes has drawn my attention to a relevant passage in Sheridan, *Speeches* (ed. 1842), i. 254.

49. Portland to Shelburne, 5th May 1782 (P.R.O., H.O. 100/1, fo. 182ᵛ).

50. Rutland to Sydney, 27th Feb. 1784 (P.R.O., H.O. 100/12, fo. 125ᵛ).

51. Rutland to Sydney, 30th Aug. 1785 (H.M.C., *Rutland*, iii. 238).

52. Edith M. Johnston, 'The state of the Irish house of commons in 1791', in *R.I.A. Proc.*, lix., sect. C. This essay was written before the publication of Dr. Johnston's book *Great Britain and Ireland, 1760–1800*, which is, however, only indirectly concerned with the main issue here discussed.

Eight

Ireland under the Union

HISTORICAL treatment of Irish political life under the union has generally been confined within a fairly narrow range of topics: the failure of the legislative union to bring about genuine integration of Great Britain and Ireland; the maintenance of the 'protestant ascendancy'; the depression and the revival of Irish nationalism; the effect of the union on the Irish economy; the influence of Irish politics in Great Britain. All these have one thing in common, a strong element of continuity with the pre-union era. With regard to the failure of integration and the maintenance of the protestant ascendancy, the truth of this is self-evident, and the same may be said with regard to the British attitude to Irish national claims. As for the nationalist movement in Ireland in the post-union era, it is clear enough that the tradition carried on by the Young Irelanders, by the Fenians, and by Sinn Fein, had its origin in the French revolutionary doctrines that inspired the leaders of the United Irishmen. When we turn to the other wing of the nationalist movement, however, the line of continuity is not quite so clear. O'Connell's vast organization almost certainly drew something from the long-standing tradition of peasant combination against landlords and tithe-proctors; but the constitutional nationalism, of which he was the first prominent exponent, though it has some obvious links with the eighteenth century, probably owes even more to the nineteenth. The history of Anglo-Irish economic and financial relations during the period of the legislative union, however we interpret it, whether we see a dark conspiracy to keep Ireland poor, or the unhappy outcome of well-meant, though misguided, policies, or the inexorable working out of forces beyond human control, is simply another chapter of an old story. There may be a diversity of incident; there is no break in the plot. Even when we move outside Ireland itself, and consider the effect of the union on British politics, we find nothing radically new. In the seventeenth and eighteenth centuries, as in the nineteenth, Irish affairs had, though much more rarely, played an important, sometimes, perhaps, a decisive part in English political life.

It would, however, be fatal to conclude that the study of Ireland under the union yields nothing new, with the exception of some elements in O'Connellite nationalism, and that the legislative union, though it strengthened some factors in Irish development and weakened others, produced no more positive result. The period between 1800 and 1920 did, in fact, witness a change, a development, in Irish history, a change that could not have come about either before the union was made, or after its dissolution, a change that, though closely linked with the political and economic factors mentioned above, has nevertheless a distinct character of its own.

What follows can best be introduced by a passage from a brilliant but half-forgotten book, A. V. Dicey's *England's Case against Home Rule*, published in 1887:

> The English connection has inevitably . . . brought upon Ireland the evils involved in the artificial suppression of revolution . . . Ireland, in short, which under English rule has lacked good administration has by the same rule been inevitably prevented from attempting the cure of deeply-rooted evils by the violent though occasionally successful remedy of revolution.

The essence of Dicey's argument lies in the phrase 'artificial suppression of revolution'. But however justly this phrase might be used to describe the effects of British policy in Ireland before 1800, or even for some decades afterwards, it cannot be denied that at the very time at which Dicey wrote Ireland was, in fact, in the middle of a revolution—political, economic, and social— which, so far from being suppressed, was being organized and carried through by the British government. By a whole series of enactments, beginning with the admission of Roman Catholics to parliament in 1829, and passing on through the reform of the electoral system, the disestablishment and disendowment of the church, and the reform of local government, to the final destructions of landlordism, there was brought about a complete change in the balance of power in Ireland. It is no exaggeration to call this change a revolution; and though government action was sometimes stimulated by violence in Ireland, the revolution itself was not a violent one; it was brought about by constitutional means and with a strongly-marked regard for existing interests. This revolution at least, then, was not suppressed; but the violent methods, the breaking up of the framework of society, the disregard for continuity of authority, the defiance of legal right—all these characteristics that so often accompany revolution were avoided.

That such a transformation of Irish society could be brought about, in such a way, under the union, and not otherwise, had been foreseen more than forty years before Dicey wrote by another observer, less accurately informed, perhaps, on the detailed history of Anglo-Irish relations, and certainly less competent to discuss the constitutional aspects of the question, but one who had the double advantage of being circumstantially detached from any partisanship in Anglo-Irish affairs, and of being more familiar than Dicey was with both the theory and the practice of revolution. In January and February 1844 Count Cavour published in the *Bibliothèque Universelle de Genève* a remarkable essay entitled 'Ireland, its Present and its Future', devoted very largely to a discussion of O'Connell's repeal movement, then at its height. Cavour's argument, briefly, is this: that the two reforms most urgently necessary in Ireland are the removal of the religious grievance by the disestablishment (though he does not use this term) of the church, and the radical adjustment of relations between landlord and tenant, in favour of the latter; that these reforms can be brought about (indeed, he thinks they will be brought about) peacefully, gradually, but effectively, by the British parliament; that if repeal were granted, O'Connell would be unable to restrain the violence of the democratic majority who would dominate the new Irish parliament, and that the same changes would be brought about abruptly, even violently, with little or no regard for vested interests, the rights of property, or even for justice.

On the church question he writes:

> The radical reform of the church not only is possible without the repeal of the union, but it is even probable . . . With a national parliament it would be more speedy and more complete; but it would probably be also violent, unjust, and perhaps cruel. If the union continues, it will be effected slowly by regular and legal means. I can understand a preference for the former course; but

whatever love of revolutions there may be, we cannot forget how costly to humanity are the sudden and violent derangements which always follow in their train.

On the land question, Cavour writes at greater length; but the essence of his argument is the same: the British government is already moving towards an effective reform of the land system; but such reform, if left to a popularly-elected Irish legislature, 'would be dictated by a spirit of reaction and vengeance, which might be as fatal to Ireland in the future, as the spirit of oppression and of intolerance has been in the past'.

We are here concerned only with Cavour's forecast of British policy, and we need not accept his opinion about the probable conduct of an Irish parliament, brought into existence by a repeal of the union. But what he says about the composition of such a parliament (or, rather, of its house of commons) is probably true; for the electoral reforms that had already taken place had brought about a shift in the balance of political power. What Cavour fails to realize (or at least to make explicit) is that even under the legislative union the influence of these reforms was powerful; and it was to become more and more powerful as the century progressed. They were themselves part of the revolutionary transformation of Irish life, and, in turn, they contributed both to the rate and to the extent of that transformation. And these electoral reforms were essentially a product of the union. The policy of enlarging the franchise was dictated by conditions in Great Britain, and was extended to Ireland simply because Ireland, as part of the United Kingdom, could not be excluded.

Cavour's prophecy that the British parliament would reform what he regarded as the greatest evils in the Irish social system was fulfilled, though not so soon as he had, perhaps, expected. The disestablishment of the church was delayed for a quarter of a century, and the effective reform of the land system even longer. The latter, when it came, went beyond what Cavour seems to have thought probable, or even desirable, and destroyed not only the excessive power of the landlords, but landlordism itself. The destruction was not merely economic, it was political and social as well. The Ballot Act of 1872 had virtually taken away what remained of the landlord's control over his tenant's vote; the establishment of local government on a popular basis had taken away his control of county affairs through the grand jury; and the break-

K

up of his estate was, in effect, the conclusion rather than the origin
of his fall from power.

The argument up to this point may be briefly summarized as
follows: that during the period of the legislative union Ireland
experienced a revolutionary change, affecting religion, property,
political power and social influence; that this change was carried
through by constitutional means, with a regard for vested interests,
and without any violent break-up of the framework of society;
that if the union had not taken place (or perhaps even if it had
come to a premature end) this change could not have come about
except by a violent upheaval and the overthrow of the old system
by force.

To this line of argument there are two objections of particular
cogency, and these must now be considered. First, it could be
argued that the legislative union was not a necessary prerequisite
of the constitutional revolution that has been described; that if
there had been no act of union in 1800, if the Irish parliament had
survived, it would, under pressure from public opinion in Ireland,
and stimulated by the example of Great Britain, have gradually
reformed itself; that with this reform of parliament would necessarily have gone a weakening of the influence of the established
church and of the landlords, leading to ecclesiastical and agrarian
measures similar to, though not necessarily identical with, those
actually passed by the British parliament. Secondly, it might be
said that the argument has been cut short at the very point at
which its falseness was about to appear. For in fact the period of
the legislative union did end in violent revolution, in the military
struggle that we euphemistically call 'The Troubles'.

These objections are very different in character: the former is a
matter of speculation, the latter, of fact. To the former, therefore,
no wholly conclusive answer can be given; yet it is the more important of the two, for if sustained it would destroy the whole case
here put forward. The latter, if not completely disposed of, might
yet be brought within the terms of a compromise.

The argument that the Irish parliament, like the British, would
have reformed itself peacefully suggests, indeed depends upon, a
comparison between political conditions in Ireland and in Great
Britain at the opening of the nineteenth century. The British
parliament, considered as a representative assembly, was, from a
modern democratic viewpoint, not much more satisfactory than

the Irish, and control over it lay in the hands of a relatively small ruling class. In the course of the century this class gradually surrendered its monopoly of power, and control over parliament passed to wider and wider sections of the population; with this development came a steady stream of other reforms, political, economic, and social, in response to the demands of the growing electorate. Why should we not suppose that the political life of Ireland would have taken a corresponding course?

Now the comparison here put forward, though specious, is misleading. Political conditions in the two kingdoms, despite some superficial resemblance, differed fundamentally in two respects, which, though closely related, are best dealt with separately.

First, there was, in British society, a kind of political gradation. It was safe for the ruling class to take into partnership, as it were, the group just on the fringe of power, and for this process to be repeated at intervals, without any sudden inrush of new forces. And while surrendering its monopoly of power, the ruling class of the pre-1832 era was able to retain for a long time a firm grip on political leadership. Even at the end of the nineteenth century the membership of the house of commons was a very imperfect reflection of the wide distribution of political power resulting from electoral reform. But the structure of Irish society offered little prospect of such a peaceful devolution of power. There was, it is true, a professional and mercantile middle class; but it was weak numerically, it was not widely distributed, and for political power it depended on alliance either with the landlords or with the masses. Later on in the century it did acquire some independent political influence, mainly as a result of reforms that it could never have won for itself. But in the critical decades after 1800 the Irish middle class was almost helpless: it might support the existing order, or it might head a revolutionary movement, as some of its members had tried to do in 1798 and 1803; it could not act as the medium for a peaceful transformation of society.

The second respect in which the Irish situation differed fundamentally from the British was in the close connexion between political power and the security of property. Such a connexion, no doubt, must always exist; and with the progressive expansion of the franchise in Great Britain there were not wanting those who foretold (not without reason) that a popularly-elected assembly would be generous in the expenditure of other men's money. But in Ireland the connexion was particularly close. The title to almost every estate in the country rested on the confiscations and settlements of the seventeenth century, which had been alternately established, reversed, and re-established, in successive parliaments. The memory of these changes was still alive, and it was impossible for an Irish landlord to view without alarm the prospect of the admission to political power of those who claimed the ownership of his estate.

The importance of this link between power and property was enormously increased by the predominantly rural character of the Irish population. In England, the force of the demand for parliamentary reform depended very largely on the growth of industrial towns, and the effect of reform was to increase the weight of urban as against rural representation. In Ireland a reform carried out on the same general principles would have had just the opposite effect: a reformed Irish parliament in the nineteenth century would have been a parliament elected, for the most part, by tenant-farmers. The Irish landlords were not always wise or well-informed, even in matters affecting their own interests; but they were not so foolish as to suppose that such a parliament would leave them in peacable possession of their estates. It is hard to believe that any argument short of force would have induced them to give up a monopoly of power which they believed to be their right and which they knew to be their security.

Two other considerations must be added to these fundamental distinctions between the British and Irish situations. First, the disruptive effect of sectarian difference, though its importance must not be exaggerated, would certainly have stood in the way of any wide extension of political power. Even among liberal-minded protestants there were many who regarded with suspicion, not unmingled with fear, the political aspirations of their Roman Catholic fellow-countrymen. Secondly, Ireland in 1800 had just emerged from an abortive attempt at revolution—the landlords victorious but frightened, the revolutionaries cowed but not reconciled. It was not, to say the least, a good starting-point for a policy of peaceful reform.

The second main objection to the argument put forward in the earlier part of this paper is that it does not take into account the violent revolution, which Ireland did in fact undergo in 1916–23. But it might fairly enough be argued that this objection is, in fact, irrelevant; for the struggle in Ireland in 1916–23 was not primarily concerned with the distribution of power or property within Ireland itself, but with the relations between Ireland and Great Britain. It was just because the internal revolution was already complete that this external, nationalist revolution could take place in isolation, uncomplicated by struggles of class and economic interests.

To express the same line of reasoning rather differently: the revolution with which Ireland seemed to be threatened in 1800 was, first, postponed by the legislative union, and then, under the shelter of that union, carried out by constitutional means. But the British government, though ready to carry out revolutionary changes in Ireland, though ready to sacrifice the church and the landlords, was not ready to sacrifice what it regarded as the national interests of England; and it was only at this point (i.e., when English interests, as distinct from the interests of any group or groups in Ireland, became involved) that violent revolution took the place of constitutional revolution. In short, the union enabled Ireland to get through one revolution peacefully, but subjected her to another revolution which was violent.

Though these two revolutions were different not only in method but in character, there is a relationship between them. It would be tempting to regard the latter simply as the completion of the former; but the facts do not warrant our assuming any such continuity in the revolutionary process. It may be that the constitutional revolution made possible the success of the nationalist revolution of 1916–23; it may be that it made some such revolution inevitable. But even if this is so, even if the constitutional revolution necessarily carried with it the dissolution of the legislative union, it was nevertheless complete in itself, and it remains the greatest monument of the union period.

Though we may thus regard the Irish revolution of 1916–23 as irrelevant to the main argument here put forward, it leads directly to discussion of a topic that may seem to deserve more attention than has yet been given in this essay—Irish nationalism. To some historians, this has been the dominant theme of the period. P. S. O'Hegarty, for example, describes his book, *Ireland under the Union*, as 'the story of a people coming out of captivity', and he makes it clear that he is thinking of political, not of economic or social, captivity. This interpretation is, no doubt, part of a great

popular myth; but if we concentrate on a comparison between the
constitutional position in 1800 and in 1922, and if we make careful
selection of events and topics in the intervening period, we can
transform it into something remarkably like history. In constitutional theory, the kingdom of Ireland, on the eve of the legislative
union, enjoyed a greater degree of independence than the Irish
Free State under the terms of the treaty settlement; but the independence of the Free State was real, and capable (as subsequent
events were to show) of expansion, while that of pre-union Ireland
was largely illusory. The Irish nationality established by the
dissolution of the union was far more effective than that destroyed
by its enactment—Grattan's rhetorical 'Ireland is now a nation'
might well seem more appropriate to 1922 than to 1782.

But this political-nationalist interpretation of Irish history between 1800 and 1922, though it can be made to appear plausible,
leaves too much out of account; it either reduces most of what
happened during the intervening period to a meaningless jumble
of events, or else imposes on those events a pattern created by the
mythologist, very different from the pattern educed from them by
the historian. The task of disentangling these patterns is made
more difficult by the fact that the mythological pattern is not just
an invention. During the greater part of the period there were two
movements to which the term 'nationalist' is commonly applied.
The older of these—the physical force revolutionary movement
derived from the United Irishmen—did in fact keep alive the
tradition of a simple political struggle between an Irish nation and
an English invader. It is this tradition that has captured popular
Irish historiography, and has not only obscured the true significance of the union period, but has tended almost to deprive it of
any significance at all. For throughout the period the revolutionary
tradition remained almost unchanged; if it acquired any new
element or new incentive this came, not from any development in
Ireland (and certainly not from the conditions produced by the
legislative union), but from the romantic nationalism of nineteenth-century Europe.

The other nationalism took its character, and perhaps its origin,
from O'Connell's campaign for repeal and may be regarded as a
distintive product of the union period. Strictly speaking, however,
it was not 'nationalist' at all: its most extreme demand was for an
Irish parliament within the British monarchy, and when it came

nearest to success, in 1912–14, it professed to be satisfied with a
settlement that would have left the basis of the union untouched.
It is significant, but not, perhaps, surprising, that in modern Irish
political hagiology the leaders of this movement have fallen into
the background. Emmet, the Young Irelanders and the Fenians—
the milestones between 1798 and 1916—occupy the centre; Butt
and Redmond (though fit subjects for Ph.D. theses) have little
popular appeal; Parnell is still a figure of controversy, and O'Connell holds his great position not as the Repealer but as the
'Liberator', the victor in the struggle for Catholic Emancipation.

But here, as so often, popular judgement is wrong. It is true
that the Irish revolution of 1916–23, which overthrew the legislative union, was inspired by the spirit of 1798, and was a deliberate
reaction against the constitutional nationalist movement, which,
from O'Connell to Redmond, was accused of having betrayed, by
its weakness, its folly and its venality, the rights of the Irish nation.
But the influence of this constitutional nationalism did not disappear with the collapse of the Home Rule party at the general
election of 1918. In the making of the Free State, the hand was the
hand of Collins, but the voice was the voice of O'Connell. It was
due mainly to the deep-seated, though hardly-realized, influence
of O'Connell, and of the movement derived from his example,
that parliamentary democracy survived in the Twenty-six
Counties. We can easily forget how precarious that survival
seemed at a time when it could be claimed that Glasnevin was
better represented in the Dail than any other part of the country, a
time when a returning officer could be forced, at the point of a
revolver, to fill up voting-papers for every elector on his list, a
time when the leader of a great party could base his policy on the
assertion that 'the majority has no right to do wrong'—an admir-
able moral principle, but one which, if acted upon by the minority,
is apt to stultify the parliamentary system. That out of such a time
there should emerge not a military dictatorship but the framework
(at least) of a democracy was, in a real sense, the achievement
of O'Connell; and that this democracy should have at its disposal
a well-established system of popular administration, and should
set out on its course without the burdens of ecclesiastical or social
privilege, was the great legacy of the union period to contemporary
Ireland.

Nine

The Church of Ireland: Disestablishment and its Aftermath

THERE have been many occasions in European history when revolutionary forces, in one country or another, have violently (or, at least, arbitrarily) deprived an established church of its privileged position and taken possession of its property. But the orderly and cautious severing of the links between church and state, with due regard to the various interests concerned, has been of less common occurrence. The Irish Church Act of 1869, apart altogether from its importance in the development of nineteenth-century Ireland, has therefore some general interest as an example of the policy of disestablishment in action.

The idea of a separation between church and state was widespread in the nineteenth century—it was, indeed, one of the 'errors' condemned by Pope Pius IX in 1864; and in the British Isles there were many who advocated disestablishment not only in Ireland but in England and Scotland as well. It is true that the Irish situation was in one respect peculiar, for the established church there was the church of only a small minority of the people. But the principle of establishment, and the legal and administrative problems involved in ending it, were the same in Ireland as elsewhere. The essence of church establishment is that the ecclesiastical law forms part of the law of the land and that, consequently, the courts of the church exercise a real jurisdiction. Public opinion, however, has generally been less concerned about the legal position than about endowment, though the latter is no necessary condition of establishment. The established church in England and Ireland was endowed both with land and with tithe; and it was widely held that these were, in fact, the property of the nation which might, if it chose, turn them to other uses. It is worth noting here that tithe, though it might have the appearance of an ecclesiastical tax (and was often so regarded) is simply a form of property; and in Ireland it did not end with disestablishment, though thereafter it was paid to the state instead of to the clergy.

This popular concentration on endowment as the essential characteristic of an established church made it even more difficult to justify the position in Ireland. To the utilitarian mind of the period it seemed an absurd anomaly. Here was a diocesan and parochial organization covering the whole country, with a hierarchy of archbishops and bishops, deans and chapters, with their ancillary officers, and hundreds of parochial clergymen, enjoying all the endowments of a national church and yet serving only some 12 per cent of the population, more than three-quarters of which were Roman Catholics and the rest protestant dissenters. It is true that in a narrowly legal and constitutional viewpoint the church's case was strong, and its position was formally secured 'for ever' by the terms of the Anglo-Irish union of 1800. But sixty years later the political situation had changed. With the progress of parliamentary reform the Irish M.P.s at Westminster had become more and more representative of public opinion in Ireland, and by the early 1860s a substantial majority of them were in favour of disestablishing and disendowing the church. It is always dangerous to regard any historical event as 'inevitable'; but it seems safe to say that by this time the days of the Irish church as an establishment were already numbered.

That the crisis came just when it did was due to Gladstone. His immediate motives lie in the political situation in 1868, when he had newly succeeded Russell in the liberal leadership. He needed a policy that would unite all sections of the party behind him, that would draw popular support from Ireland and that would force the conservatives to fight on dangerous ground. Disestablishment met these three requirements; and Gladstone went into battle with all his usual zest and with his usual firm conviction that this skilfully-organized manoeuvre was the fulfilment of a high moral purpose. The manoeuvre was at any rate successful; and the election of 1868 brought him into office with a large majority.

This is not the place to follow out in detail the preparation and the passage through parliament of the Irish Church Act of 1869; but some general comments must be made. Considered simply as a piece of legislation it might well be regarded as Gladstone's most striking achievement. He had no precedent to work by, for no such transaction had been carried through before; and his surviving papers bear witness to the thoroughness with which he set about the task and the immense difficulties it presented. He was guided throughout by two main principles. The first was a scrupulous regard for personal interests: every individual, clerical or lay, deriving an income from church property, must be assured of adequate compensation. The second principle was less precise but (at least in Gladstone's eyes) no less important: the future of the disestablished church must be cared for; it would lose its property and its privileged position in relation to the state, but it must be enabled to continue as a voluntary society.

In seeking to preserve these principles Gladstone had to face some difficulties. Many of his supporters cared little for the vested interests of churchmen and nothing at all for the future of the church; and with a vast reform programme before him he could not afford to alienate them by appearing too conciliatory. But his caution was exercised in the presentation of the bill rather than in its drafting; and the two basic principles remained intact. As for the conservative opposition, it was outvoted in the commons; and the conservative leaders, though they had a strong majority in the lords, dared not use it to defeat the clearly-expressed will of the electorate. On 26th July 1869 the Irish Church Act received the royal assent.

The effect of the measure, briefly stated, was twofold. First, it severed the connexion between church and state, as from 1st January 1871, and enacted that the ecclesiastical law of Ireland should, from that date, cease to exist as law. This was the essence of disestablishment. Secondly, it confiscated all ecclesiastical property, except for churches actually in use and their adjoining churchyards, and placed it in the hands of a body of commissioners, who were to be responsible for satisfying, out of this property, the life interests of all those who had derived any income from it. Such payments, however, were made conditional upon the continued performance of the appropriate duties; and thus the church was, in a sense, temporarily re-endowed with the remaining life-service of its clergy and of its lay officials.

To Irish churchmen at the time disestablishment and dis-endowment seemed a crushing disaster, an act of national apostasy of which they were the principal victims:

Darkly dawns the New Year
On a churchless nation

ran the opening lines of an anthem written for use in Derry
cathedral on 1st January 1871. It was hardly surprising that Gladstone should have been regarded as the main villain; yet had
churchmen but taken time to reflect they might have realized that
his careful framing of the act had smoothed the path of reconstruction that they were now obliged to tread. The real danger to
the church did not lie in loss of status and property, but in the
internal weaknesses and disunity that the new situation both revealed and exacerbated. That these weaknesses were, in large
measure, overcome and the organic unity of the church not only
preserved but strengthened, owed a great deal to Gladstone's
foresight.

In the first place, the act made careful provision for the continuation of the church as a voluntary society. Though the ecclesiastical law ceased to exist as part of the law of the land, it was to be
deemed binding on members of the church in the same manner
as if they had mutually contracted to accept and observe it; and it
could be enforced in relation to any property vested in the church
as if it has been conveyed upon trust to be enjoyed by persons who
should observe that law. Further, the act authorized the bishops,
clergy and laity to set up a constitutional body to legislate for the
church; and laws made by this body would have the same con-
tractual force as the ecclesiastical law actually existing at the time
of disestablishment.

The enormous advantage of these provisions was recognized by
Archbishop Trench of Dublin, much as he deplored the whole
policy of the act:

> The one great merit which the scheme possesses, and I acknow-
> ledge it a very great one, is that it will not now require acts of ours
> to put us in communion in doctrine and discipline with the
> Church of England, and with our own Church and the past; but
> that, on the contrary, it will require distinct acts of ours to put us
> out of fellowship with that church, and to break our continuity
> and connection with our own past.

For a time, it might have seemed that Trench was being too
optimistic. The formal continuity of the church was provided for,
and its power of self-government assured: but might not this very
power destroy that continuity? Trench himself had foreseen the

danger as early as April 1868. Irish churchmen in general tended
to be strongly 'protestant'; and Trench feared that disestablishment might be followed by an attempt to set up 'a new church,
which shall have purged the prayer-book of the popish leaven
which taints it still'. William Magee, bishop of Peterborough, an
Irishman who had been promoted to the English bench from the
deanery of Cork, was more explicit in his fears: he saw the 'rocks'
ahead as 'liturgical revision', 'lay tyranny' and 'schism between
north and south'.

The fears of both men were realized, though not to anything
like the extent that their gloomier predictions had suggested; and
it was almost inevitable that something of the sort should happen.
Before disestablishment the Irish church lacked any means of
forming or expressing a corporate view. Indeed, as a distinct
national church it had lost its constitutional existence with the act
of union of 1800: thereafter, it was merely two provinces of the
'United Church of England and Ireland', an institution that had
no being save in the minds of lawyers and on the title page of the
prayer-book. There was, in theory, an Irish convocation, but it
had not met since the reign of Queen Anne; and the church could
speak, if at all, only through the doubtful medium of informal
episcopal meetings. Disestablishment called into being, for the
first time, representative assemblies of clergy and laity; and
these, together with the bishops, formed a 'General Convention', which met in Dublin in February 1870 to prepare the way
for the coming change by giving the church a constitution.
In such a body, at such a period, there were bound to be demands for change; and controversy, however regrettable, was
not to be avoided.

The main controversy took the form foreseen by Trench and
Magee. Disestablishment had made prayer-book revision possible,
and there was a powerful party determined to make it effective.
In this, it is fair to say, Irish opinion merely reflected English. The
revision of the canons and rubrics, completed by 1877, had for its
prime object to freeze liturgical practice as it stood, in Ireland and
England alike, before the influence of the ritualist movement had
begun to affect it; and this was, in substance, the end aimed at,
though not attained, in England by the Public Worship Regula-
tion Act of 1874. The Irish measures, however unpalatable to
some, were effective because they represented the free decision of

an ecclesiastical assembly, not the policy imposed by a secular parliament. The self-government that came with disestablishment had certainly brought with it the threat of disruption; but the very fact of self-government had made it possible for people to accept compromise with a good conscience.

But there was a second way also in which the terms of the church act helped to preserve unity. It is realistic, without being cynical, to recognize that its financial provisions were a powerful factor in holding the church together. Every clergyman was entitled to a life annuity, equal to the income of his office or benefice, payable out of the confiscated church property; and in return for this annuity he was to continue to perform his ecclesiastical duties. But the act also provided that an annuitant might have his annuity commuted for a lump sum, which would then be paid over to a 'Church representative body' (established under the act), and this body would thereafter be responsible for paying him. The vast majority of the clergy agreed to commute; and the fact that, as a result they were receiving their incomes from a church authority and not (as might have been the case) from a government department, undoubtedly tended to strengthen their solidarity and to make for unity.

In another way also the financial position had an influence, which it is easier to recognize than to measure, on the structure of the disestablished church. The fact that the life service of the existing clergy was assured gave a breathing-space; but it was no more than a breathing-space. The sum handed over to the representative body, under the commutation system, was so calculated that both capital and interest would be exhausted when the last annuitant died, and the interval must be used for the accumulation of fresh capital, so that the income of succeeding clergy might be assured. Clearly, the church must look to the laity, and especially to the wealthier laity, for this new capital. It is to the credit of the laity that they responded generously, and the finances of the church were put on a firm basis; but it can hardly be doubted that awareness of this dependence on lay support had some effect on the attitudes of both clergy and laity in the formulation of church policy, and particularly in the controversy over prayer-book revision. Magee's fear of 'lay tyranny' proved to be exaggerated; but lay influence in matters that some clergy regarded as their own exclusive concern was almost certainly strengthened by the fact that the church was now, for the first time, financially dependent on the voluntary support of its members.

When we turn from the financial to the constitutional aspect of reconstruction we find the influence of the laity more direct and obvious. The church act had authorized the bishops, clergy and laity to elect representatives to a synod or convention. This inclusion of the laity may have been merely permissive, though contemporary lawyers interpreted it as mandatory; but, in any case, the laity would certainly have been called in, as they had been in other self-governing branches of the Anglican communion. And the laity naturally took a leading part in the framing of a constitution. Many of them were members of one or other house of parliament, and many had had legal training. The influence of this kind of experience can be seen in the constitution that emerged. The general synod (the supreme governing body of the church) is not divided into houses, sitting separately, on the model of Westminster, but the legislative procedure is, in other respects, almost an exact replica of British parliamentary practice. The procedure, however appropriate in its original setting, is hardly suitable for an assembly that meets only once a year, and then for less than a week; but it reflects the status and the outlook of the men who framed the constitution.

Though the rules of legislative procedure thus bear a clear mark of lay influence, the constitution as a whole was carefully balanced. Clergy and laity were to sit together in a house of representatives, but their separate rights were safeguarded by a provision for voting by orders upon the requisition of ten members. The house of bishops, voting separately, might veto any proposed measure but in certain circumstances this veto was restricted: if a measure rejected by the bishops were, at the next ordinary meeting of the synod, reaffirmed by a two-thirds majority of the clergy and laity (voting conjointly or by orders), the veto would lapse unless sustained by at least two-thirds of the bishops. In general, one may say that the constitution represented something of a compromise. The laity were clearly determined to establish their right to a substantial share in the government of the church, and in this they succeeded; but the result as it worked out, hardly amounted to the 'lay tyranny' of which Magee had been afraid.

As one looks back on the Irish Church Act after the lapse of a century it no longer appears the disaster it seemed to contemporaries. By that time the connexion between church and state had lost much of its meaning. In matters connected with religion, and especially in the field of education, the government had long followed a neutral policy; establishment conferred little more than a rather faded prestige; and the endowment that accompanied it often exposed the church to damaging attack. In retrospect, the surprising thing is not that the establishment came to an end when it did, but rather that it should have lasted so long. An institution so uncongenial to the reforming mind of the nineteenth century could hardly hope to survive; and it was of immense advantage to the church that the blow was not deferred; half a generation later, it would have been much more destructive. By that time the land-lord class, the main support of the church in many rural areas, was already in retreat; the presence of a militant and well-organized Irish nationalist party at Westminster would have made the com-parative moderation of Gladstone's measure difficult, if not im-possible; and in the bitter home rule conflict that gripped the whole country Magee's prophecy of a 'schism between north and south' might well have come true. As it was, the church had time to reconstruct its organization and to adapt itself to changing political and social conditions. The unity that grew out of this difficult period has proved strong enough to survive revolution, civil war and political partition of the country.

Ten

Carson—Unionist and Rebel

WHEN I was a boy, growing up in Belfast, few names were so commonly in men's mouths as that of Edward Carson. Adored by one section of the population, hated (I think I may say) by another, he was known to all.

> Sir Edward Carson had a cat
> That sat upon a stool,
> And every time it caught a rat
> It shouted: No Home Rule!

That scrap of rhyme—better, perhaps, than any long exposition —sums up what we, as children, knew of Carson and of what he stood for. And I suppose that it still sums up Carson for most of those who think about him at all—he was the man who led the Ulster protestants in their campaign against the home rule policy of the Irish nationalists and the British liberals.

This popular summary of Carson's outlook and career is both inadequate and misleading: inadequate, because he was much more than just the champion of protestant Ulster; misleading, because, at bottom, the fate of Ulster (or of any section of Ulster) was not his main concern. The fact that Carson's name today is so inseparably linked with the north-east is evidence not of his success, but of his failure.

To make these points clear, it is necessary to set Carson's participation in the 'Ulster Question' in its proper perspective. It was, after all, only one episode in a long and full life. His professional career spanned more than half a century: he was called to the Irish bar in 1877, and retired from his position as a lord of appeal in 1929. For the greater part of this period he was constantly active in politics. He became M.P. for Dublin University in 1892; and even after he went to the house of lords, as a judge, in 1921, he continued to intervene, from time to time, on political questions. Against this background, his special connexion with Ulster seems relatively short. It lasted, in fact, for little more than a decade—from February 1910 to February 1921. It is, of course, true that many a great man's claim to be remembered rests on the events of a much briefer period. But in this case the question is not just one of time. Carson in 1910, before he had established any close connexion with the north of Ireland—before, indeed, he had any wide reputation there—was already a leading figure in British political life. And it is safe to say that even if what we call the 'Ulster question' had never existed, Carson would still have had an important place in the legal and political history of the early twentieth century.

Carson had entered politics under the patronage of Arthur Balfour. His courage and skill as a crown prosecutor had made a great impression on Balfour, who was Irish chief secretary from 1887 to 1891; and it was Balfour who secured his appointment as solicitor-general for Ireland in 1892. But once Carson was in parliament, and in London, he showed that he could stand on his own feet. His maiden speech in the house of commons established almost immediately his position in the conservative party, and in 1900 he became solicitor-general for England. His professional progress was no less remarkable. Within a few years he had become one of the leaders of the English bar—by 1899 his fees amounted to £20,000 a year; in an age of great advocates—Sir Edward Clarke, Marshall Hall, Rufus Isaacs, F. E. Smith—he was regarded by many as the greatest of them all.

When the conservatives went out of office in 1905 Carson was already one of the leading members of the party. The general election of 1906 improved his political prospects, for it seriously weakened the conservative front bench, and enhanced Carson's importance among the survivors. From this time onwards he was one of the small inner group that directed the party's fortunes, and a figure of national importance in British politics. It may be an exaggeration to say, as one of his biographers has said, that he could have had the conservative leadership (and with it the prospect of becoming one day prime minister) almost for the asking; but his influence in the party was certainly so great that no leader could have felt secure in face of his opposition.

It was this influence in the conservative party, and especially among the back-benchers, that made Carson such an important political force during the first world war. His importance during this period was, perhaps, more immediately obvious to contemporaries than it is to us today, for he did not play any decisive part in the administration of affairs. He did, indeed, hold high office. When the purely liberal ministry gave way to a coalition, in the spring of 1915, Carson became attorney-general; but he resigned a few months later; and though he came in again under Lloyd George, in December 1916, as first lord of the admiralty, and entered the war cabinet in July 1917, he was neither happy nor particularly effective as a minister. Lloyd George, in his *War Memoirs*, accounted for this by the fact that Carson was an Irishman, asserting that all Irishmen are naturally opposed to every government, even one supported by their own party. Though we need not accept this somewhat brash explanation, Carson's strength certainly lay in his power of criticism. He had withdrawn from the first coalition government, in October 1915, because he was dissatisfied with its conduct of the war; and after that he became its most effective critic in the house of commons. Other critics could be silenced or ignored, but not Carson, whose skill in debate and obvious sincerity won for him increasing support from back-bench conservatives. The consequent threat to the position of the conservative members of the cabinet helped to bring about the crisis of December 1916, in which Asquith was overthrown and Lloyd George established in his place. There is no need here to go into the details of that complicated and controversial transaction; but accounts by those who took part show clearly enough the decisive character of Carson's influence; and, when it was over, he emerged, with Lloyd George and Bonar Law, as one of 'the new triumvirate' (to quote Sir Winston Churchill) who 'assumed, with what were in practice dictatorial powers, the direction of affairs'. But the influence exercised in opposition did not survive in office; and though Carson could never become a negligible figure, by the end of the war he was on the fringe of British politics rather than at the centre.

Though Carson thus holds a secure place in what we may call the main stream of British political history, his basic interest, from first to last, lay in his own country—'It is only for Ireland that I'm in politics', he told Arthur Balfour in 1900. His duty to Ireland, as he saw it, was to maintain intact the parliamentary union with Great Britain. He had started life as a liberal, and in some respects he remained a liberal to the end; but in the home rule crisis of 1886 he followed Chamberlain and the liberal-unionists. At that time he had no thought of going into parliament himself (the height of his ambition was a county court judgeship), but he supported unionist candidates in Dublin city and county in the general election of 1886. When he did enter parliament, eight years later, his overriding political purpose was to save the union. To this, he was prepared to sacrifice everything else—party allegiance, political alliances, personal friendships, his own prospects of promotion. In 1896, for example, when the conservatives had just returned to power and when he could confidently hope for office and advancement, he quarrelled with the government, and even became temporarily estranged from his friend and patron, Balfour, over an Irish land bill. He believed that this measure was unjust to the landlords, whom he regarded as one of the main bulwarks of the union, and he denounced 'the everlasting attempt to make peace in Ireland by giving sops to one party at the expense of the other'. This quarrel was later made up; but it provides an early example of Carson's refusal to abandon principle for the sake of party; more than twenty years later, it was on an Irish issue that he resigned from the war cabinet, in February 1918. 'I am re- lost solved,' he said when he refused the conservative whip in 1896, 'to seat take whatever course is best for Ireland.' There could be no doubt in his mind that the best course for Ireland was to remain within the United Kingdom; and it was this conviction that led him to accept, in February 1910, the leadership of the Irish unionist M.P.s at Westminster.

Carson's special connexion with Ulster politics begins at this point; but it would be a mistake to suppose that he deliberately set himself at the head of an exclusively Ulster movement. Though the Irish unionist M.P.s, about twenty strong, represented (with very few exceptions) Ulster constituencies, their policy, like that of the British conservative party to which they belonged, was not to get special treatment for Ulster, but to defeat home rule completely and to keep the whole of Ireland within the United Kingdom. It was because he believed that Ulster unionists could play a decisive part in this campaign that Carson concentrated attention on the north.

At this point, the campaign was going badly for the unionists. The general election of January 1910 had left Asquith's liberal government dependent for its majority on Redmond and the Irish nationalists; and there could be no doubt that Redmond would now compel the liberals to fulfil their long-standing promise to bring in a home rule bill. The bill could, of course, be rejected by the house of lords, as had happened in 1893; but the government was determined to destroy the lords' veto on legislation; and, once that had been done, what could prevent the passage of a home rule act? The only chance for the unionists lay in a swing of public opinion in Britain; but another general election, in December 1910, left the parliamentary position unchanged, and enabled the government to pass the parliament act, by which the power of the lords was reduced—they could hold up a bill for two years, after which it could become law without their consent. This victory for the liberal-Irish nationalist alliance removed the last constitutional barrier to home rule, but it only made the unionists more determined than ever in their opposition. Despite their failure in the election of December 1910, they still believed that British public opinion would support them against home rule, and they bent all their efforts to force a dissolution of parliament and a new appeal to the country.

Carson had taken a leading part in opposing the parliament act; and after it was passed he believed, like the other unionist leaders, that it would still be possible to raise public opposition to home rule to such a pitch that the government would not dare to proceed without another general election. We might say that he regarded the British public as a jury, from which it was his business to get a favourable verdict. And just as, in the conduct of a case, his practice was to fasten on one crucial point, and let the decision stand or fall by that, so now he concentrated all his argument on the position of the Ulster protestants.

From Carson's point of view, this concentration on Ulster offered a double advantage. First, it provided useful material out of which to fashion a case for the British public. If the liberals laid stress on the moral claim of the majority in Ireland, the unionists could bring forward the moral claim of the majority in Ulster—they always kept carefully in the background the statistical fact that this majority was a very slender one, and they constantly spoke as if the inhabitants of the province were solidly protestant and unionist. At a period when protestant sentiment and imperial pride were still strong in Britain, the picture of empire-loving protestants being handed over to the tyranny of Rome and the oppressive rule of Irish separatists could be safely counted on to make an impression upon British voters—even among liberals it was not without effect. Secondly, and this was much more important, Carson was absolutely convinced that home rule, with Ulster left out, simply would not work, and that Redmond would never accept it. If, therefore, he could show, beyond possibility of doubt, that the Ulster unionist slogan 'We will not have home rule' meant what it said, and that no act of parliament would make any difference, then (he believed) home rule would be killed stone dead—and to kill home rule was the governing purpose of his life.

All Carson's activities in Ulster between 1911 and 1914 must be seen in the light of this single purpose. To most contemporaries he appeared as the leader of a local separatist movement; and some historians have seen him in the same character. And it is true, of course, that much of what he said and did during the period seems to fit this interpretation. But behind all and inspiring all was his determination to smash home rule; for him Ulster was an argument, not an end in itself. It could, indeed, hardly be otherwise. Carson was not an Ulsterman, but a southerner: by birth, tradition, education and family connexion he belonged to the unionist minority that had carried on into the twentieth century the spirit and outlook of the old protestant ascendancy. 'He has no country, only a caste,' said one of his critics, and the gibe has some truth in it; but for Carson it was the caste to which he belonged that made his country worth serving, and he could see only a black future if that caste were destroyed.

It was, then, to save the whole of Ireland from what he regarded as certain disaster that Carson committed himself so completely to the Ulster unionists, and encouraged and directed their plans to resist the authority of the British parliament. The combination was one of mutual advantage. The Ulster unionists had hitherto carried little weight at Westminster—their tory allies had used them and despised them; Carson's leadership now gave them a standing and an influence that they had never known before. And for Carson, as has been said, Ulster resistance was the weapon that was to kill home rule.

The relationship between Carson and the Ulster unionists presented to the world a picture of boundless devotion on one side and unquestioned authority on the other—in public, the vast crowds that came to his meetings listened to him with a kind of religious awe; in private conclaves with the local leaders his decisions and instructions were accepted automatically, and nothing was finally settled until 'Sir Edward' had given the word. But it must always be remembered that Carson had not created the movement that he now ruled so effectively. He had come to it from the outside; and though he had given it prestige and cohesion, it still retained an independent force of its own. There is, indeed, a sense in which Carson became the prisoner, rather than the leader of, the Ulster unionists. By the logic of his case, he must back to the uttermost their preparations to resist home rule. All these preparations were based on the assumption that they might have to resist by force, to stand alone and fight for their own land. They set up a provisional government, to take over the province of Ulster the moment a home rule act came into operation; they made plans for financial and economic administration; they raised, trained and equipped 100,000 men to guard the border and prevent internal disturbance. John Redmond described these preparations as 'a gigantic game of bluff and blackmail'. There is no evidence of bluff; but there was certainly a form of blackmail—a demand, under threat of civil war, that Ulster should be excluded from any scheme of home rule. Such exclusion would carry with it, as a natural corollary, the establishment of home rule in the other three provinces; and though this ran directly counter to Carson's declared policy, and to his own inner convictions, he was now so deeply committed to the Ulster unionists that he could not avoid supporting their demand. It is true that in doing so he made clear his continuing opposition to home rule, in any form, for any part of Ireland; and it is true also that he still believed that home rule for Ireland, without Ulster, was impracticable; but one can hardly help feeling that in the argument over exclusion, in 1913, it was the narrow, self-regarding unionism of the north-east, rather than the wider Irish unionism in which Carson had been brought up, that dominated the scene.

It is possible that by this time Carson himself was beginning to change; though, as will appear later, the change did not go very deep. Since the early 1890s he had been living in England, and his first-hand knowledge of the Irish political conditions, apart from those of Ulster, was growing out of date. He maintained some contact with the scattered unionists of the south and west; but he hardly realized as clearly as when he had lived with them how difficult and precarious was their position. 'They are so different from the north of Ireland and do so little for themselves,' he complained in November 1913, not pausing to ask what they *could* do. About the same time, he put his position bluntly to a group of southern unionist delegates: 'If I win in Ulster,' he asked them, 'am I to refuse the fruits of victory because you have lost?' They answered 'No'; but it is the question, not the answer, that matters. In Carson's mind, exclusion was ceasing to be merely a tactical trick and was becoming a policy, a second-best alternative, no doubt, but still a positive policy. And to make that policy work he would, if necessary, leave the southern unionists to their fate. It was a realistic decision: Carson the advocate was saving what could be saved for his clients. But it was a decision to which Carson the man never became heartily reconciled.

The onset of the European war, in August 1914, postponed the final settlement; and when the home rule question again became urgent, in 1916, the situation had been radically changed. So far as Carson was concerned, however, it was not the insurrection of Easter Week that made the difference. He had always been convinced that the Irish home rulers, despite their constitutional methods and the apparent moderation of their aims, were at heart separatists, enemies of Britain and of the empire; the events of Easter Week could do no more than intensify his original suspicions of any system of Irish self-government. What weighed most with him in 1916 was the military situation in Europe. For a long time he had been pressing relentlessly for a more vigorous prosecution of the war—to this, everything else must give way: 'If the war is lost,' he cried in May 1916, 'we are all lost.' By this time it seemed likely that the war would be lost unless the allies could get more help from America, and American opinion was demanding loudly that something should be done to pacify Ireland. It was in these circumstances that Carson agreed to the immediate establishment of home rule, with the exclusion of the six north-eastern counties; and he carried through 'the very painful and difficult task' (as he described it) of inducing the Ulster unionists to surrender Cavan, Donegal and Monaghan, despite the fact that they were pledged, by their 'Solemn League and Covenant' of 1912, to resist home rule in any part of the province. This scheme broke down; but the pattern of partition had grown sharper. Carson and the Ulster unionists were virtually committed to accepting home rule for twenty-six counties; their task now was to make sure that the remaining six were not forced to come in also, and their determination on this point contributed to the failure of the Irish Convention of 1917.

These abortive negotiations marked a clear separation between Carson and the southern unionists. He showed this openly in the general election of 1918, when he abandoned his seat for Dublin University, which he had held for twenty-six years, and was elected instead for the Duncairn division of Belfast—for the first time the leader of the Ulster unionists sat for an Ulster constituency. But Carson was not to hold his position much longer. A little more than two years later, in February 1921, he relinquished the leadership he had held for eleven years. His action did not indicate any change of attitude on either side, but arose from the circumstances of the time: the Government of Ireland Act of 1920 had secured to the Ulster protestants the special treatment they had for so long demanded; and Carson, now well over sixty and in poor health, left it to younger men to build up the newly-established government of Northern Ireland.

The act of 1920 did not give Ireland peace, but it brought the long struggle against home rule to a formal conclusion: it was now clear to everyone that all Ireland, whether under one government or two, whether inside or outside the United Kingdom, was to have self-government. But the nature and extent of that self-government had still to be decided, and 1921 was a year of hard fighting and hard bargaining. Throughout it all, the Ulster unionists stuck fast to one point—they would never surrender the position they had secured under the Government of Ireland Act. Their old slogans against home rule, now out of date, were to be replaced by another, no less trenchantly self-confident: 'What we have, we hold.' And so long as they could hold what they had, they were increasingly disposed to let the rest of Ireland go its own way. But Carson's position was rather different. He had accepted, though he had not voted for, the act of 1920, and he supported vigorously the claims of Northern Ireland to retain its position under that act; but he could not, as the northern unionists were willing to do, write off the rest of Ireland. They, after all, had won a victory, an imperfect victory, perhaps, but still a victory. But Carson had been defeated. He had set out to save all Ireland for the union, and he had failed. His speech during the Treaty debate in the house of lords shows in almost every sentence the bitterness of helpless, hopeless, irretrievable defeat. It is a powerful piece of invective, but it contains no shred of constructive policy; and though there is a good deal about Ulster, it is essentially the reaction of a southern unionist, forced at last to realize that England has once more deserted her friends and that the days of the ascendancy are over.

It is this aspect of the speech that is of prime importance in the present context. Politically, Carson had moved away from the southern unionists (it is significant that Lord Midleton, generally regarded as their leader at this time, supported the ratification of the Treaty that Carson so fiercely opposed), but he could not shed the tradition in which he had been brought up. Though he had led the Ulster unionists, and though he constantly referred to them as 'my people', he never, in fact, became one of them. He was born, and remained throughout his life, an Irishman. T. M. Healy once said of him, 'Although a unionist, he was never un-Irish'; and this is true, though Carson himself would have rejected Healy's implied conflict between being Irish and being a unionist. His conviction that the maintenance of the union was the best thing for Ireland was perfectly genuine. And equally genuine were his efforts to promote Irish welfare; they did not spring from any notion of 'killing home rule with kindness', but from his own knowledge of the needs of the country. This is nowhere more evident than in his attitude to the controversy over university education. He was a strong and consistent supporter of Roman Catholic claims: 'I often think,' he told the house of commons in 1898, 'that members of this house, who meet habitually in England, do not thoroughly understand that the Irish Catholics are a people passionately devoted to their religion . . . what can be the use of believing that the aims of university education should be the idea of secularism, when the great bulk of the Catholic people of Ireland will not accept, and could not accept, that solution?' And even when in office, he maintained the same cause, in defiance of government policy. It is important to remember that, although so much of Carson's political life was spent in opposing what most Irishmen wanted, his attitude to Ireland had a positive as well as a negative side.

One might say, at the risk of a paradox, that Carson was a patriot, without being a nationalist. The welfare of Ireland was the guiding motive of his whole career, but he denied completely the existence of a distinct Irish nationality in any political sense. This was the position into which the Anglo-Irish minority had been virtually forced by the parliamentary union with Britain. If that union had worked out as satisfactorily as the union between Scotland and England, then most Irishmen might well have come to share the same outlook. But nineteenth-century developments produced a very different result: the minority remained a minority, increasingly isolated from the bulk of the population, increasingly dependent on Britain. What Carson failed to realize in time was that Britain could not be depended on. The protestants of the north-east took a juster, if narrower, view of the situation, and made the best terms they could for themselves. In helping them to do so, Carson only encouraged the development of a more militant Irish nationalism and hastened the establishment of an Irish republic. Today, his massive statue, more than life-size, stands defiantly before the Parliament House at Stormont. It is, one might think, an oddly-placed memorial to one who so fiercely opposed home rule and who represented an Irish rather than an Ulster tradition. For Carson was the last great figure in the long line of Anglo-Irish statesmen, and it was his fate to encounter the tragic climax of the political dilemma that each of them in turn had faced and failed to solve.

Index of Names

Abercorn, John James Hamilton, 9th earl and 1st marquess of, 138

America, 128, 129, 167

Anglesey, Arthur Annesley, 1st earl of, 71, 73

Anne, Queen, 88, 99, 103, 104, 106, 128, 156

Antrim (county), 29, 122

Arlington, Henry Bennet, earl of, 71, 73, 74, 76, 78

Armagh (county), 43; (diocese), 51, 100

Ashe, St. George, bp. of Clogher, 97

Asquith, Henry Herbert, 163

Atterbury, Francis, 102

Bagwell, Richard, 48

Balfour, Arthur James, 161, 162, 163

Barrington, Sir Jonah, 18, 19

Bathurst, Allen Bathurst, 1st Earl, 126

Belfast, 38, 67, 160, 168

Belfast Lough, 38, 67

Bellings, Richard, 48

Belturbet, 105

Benburb, 32, 61, 62

Beresford, John, 136–7

Berkeley, Charles Berkeley, 2nd earl of, 115

Berkeley of Stratton, John Berkeley, 1st Baron, 70, 81, 83

Bettesworth, Richard, 121

Blair, Robert, 31

Blood, Thomas, 33, 35

Bohemia, 18

Bolton, John, 90

Bonnel, James, 97

Bothwell Brig, 39, 43, 44

Bourke, Thomas, 45

Boyle, Michael, abp. successively of Dublin and Armagh; lord chancellor of Ireland, 43, 74, 91, 92

Bruce, Edward, 26

Bruce, Michael, 35

Brussels, 74

Buckingham, George Villiers, 2nd duke of, 71, 72, 73, 74

Buckinghamshire, John Hobart, 2nd earl of, 126

Burke, Edmund, 129

Burlington, Richard Boyle, 1st earl of, 43

Burnet, Alexander, abp. of Glasgow, 35

Burnet, Gilbert, bp. of Salisbury, 105, 112

Butler, W. F. T., 61

Butt, Isaac, 151

Butterfield, Sir Herbert, 123

Campbell, Sir John, 27

Canterbury, 92

Capel, Sir Henry, 78, 81, 97

Carlisle, Francis Howard, 5th earl of, 130, 133

Carrickfergus, 32, 38

Carson, Sir Edward (later Baron Carson of Duncairn), 160–70 *passim*

Carte, Thomas, 47, 82

Castlehaven, James Touchet, 3rd earl of, 61

Castlereagh, Robert Stewart, Viscount, 137
Cavan (county), 53, 167
Chamberlain, Joseph, 163
Charles I, 57, 61
Charles II, 36, 37, 67, 70, 71, 73, 74, 75, 78, 79, 88, 98, 101
Churchill, Sir Winston, 162
Clanricard, Ulick de Burgh, 5th earl of, 54
Clarendon, Edward Hyde, 1st earl of, 70, 71
Clarendon, Henry Hyde, 2nd earl of, 70, 81, 87
Clarke, Sir Edward, 161
Cleveland, Barbara Villiers, duchess of, 75
Clogher (diocese), 96
Coffey, Diarmid, 48
Collins, Michael, 151
Connaught, 43, 61
Conway, Edward Conway, 1st earl of, 38, 41, 69, 76, 77–8
Coote, Sir Charles, 61
Cork (diocese), 156
Coventry, Henry, 78
Cox, Sir Richard, 11, 89
Crofty Hill, 49
Cromwell, Oliver, 31
Crookshank, John, 35
Curtis, Edmund, 26

Danby, Thomas Osborne, earl of, 42, 76, 77, 78, 80
Darcy, Patrick, 55
De la Monnerie, 61
Derry (diocese), 37, 90, 91, 92, 94, 95, 96, 155
Desborough, John, 33
Dicey, A. V., 143, 144
Donaghadee, 30, 41
Donegal (county), 167
Donelan, James, 47, 59
Dopping, Anthony, bp. of Meath, 91
Down (county), 28–9
Down and Connor (diocese), 93, 94, 95, 96

Drogheda, 105
Dromore (diocese), 95
Dublin, 17, 30, 33, 41, 59, 60, 78, 83, 93, 98, 99, 100, 101, 104, 111, 120, 128, 129, 134, 138, 156, 163

Edinburgh, 41
Elizabeth, Queen, 17, 26
Emmet, Robert, 151
England, 11, 13, 14, 17, 18, 19, 20, 22, 23, 24, 27, 34, 41, 54, 55, 56, 57, 58, 62, 67, 69, 81, 83, 88, 89, 92, 93, 98, 100, 101, 103, 104, 106, 107, 117, 121, 123–39 passim, 148, 149, 152, 156, 157, 166
Essex, Arthur Capel, earl of, 37, 38, 41, 43, 70, 75–9, 80, 81, 82

Faughart, 26
Fenians, 142, 151
Ferns (diocese), 90, 94
Fitzgibbon, John (later earl of Clare), 136–7
Fitzwilliam, William Wentworth Fitzwilliam, 2nd Earl, 136
Flood, Henry, 136
Foley, Samuel, bp. of Down and Connor, 94
Foster, John, 127
Fox, Charles James, 129, 133, 134, 135, 136
Foy, Nathaniel, bp. of Waterford, 90–6 passim
France, 13, 19, 22

Galloway, 37, 44, 79
Gilbert, Sir John, 47
Gladstone, William Ewart, 153, 154, 155
Glasnevin, 151
Godolphin, Francis, 81
Gormanston, Nicholas Preston, 6th Viscount, 49, 54
Gowans, Thomas, 44

Hackett, Thomas, bp. of Down and Connor, 37, 95
Hall, Marshall, 161

Hamilton, William Douglas, 3rd duke of, 39
Hamilton, Sir Hans, 43
Hamilton, James, 28
Harbord, William, 77, 78, 81
Harcourt, Simon Harcourt, 1st Earl, 129
Harley, Robert (later earl of Oxford), 118
Healy, Timothy Michael, 169
Heckscher, Eli, 13
Henry II, 15, 16, 19, 56
Henry VII, 57
Henry VIII, 57
Hillsborough, Wills Hill, 1st earl of, 134
Houston, David, 35
Hungary, 18

Inchiquin, Murrough O'Brien, 1st earl of, 81
Irish Free State, 151
Isaacs, Rufus, 161
Islay, 27

James VI and I, 26
James VII and II, 41, 62, 87, 88
Jones, Roger, 33

Kavanagh, Stanislaus, 47
Kells, 51
Kildare, Gerald Fitzgerald, 8th earl of, 17
Kilkenny, 50, 51, 59, 61
King William, successively bp. of Derry and abp. of Dublin, 87–104 passim, 112
King's County, 60

Lambeg, 38
Laracor, 90
Laud, William, abp. of Canterbury, 31
Lauderdale, John Maitland, 1st duke of, 35, 36, 38, 39, 42, 44, 70, 80
Law, Andrew Bonar, 162
Lecky, W. E. H., 20, 21, 106
Leighton, Sir Ellis, 83

Leighton, Robert, abp. of Glasgow, 36
Leinster, 60
Lisburn, 37
Lille, 54
Lloyd George, David, 162
London, 29, 39, 42, 72, 74, 81, 104, 128, 134
Londonderry (county), 43
Louth (county), 61
Ludlow, Edmund, 33

MacNeill, Eoin, 15
Magee, William, successively bp. of Peterborough and abp. of York, 156, 157, 158, 159
Marsh, Narcissus, abp. of Dublin, 93, 98
Mary II, 88, 92, 94
Massereene, John Skeffington, 2nd Viscount, 97
Mazzini, Giuseppe, 61
Meath (diocese), 90, 91, 95
Meehan, C. P., 47, 48, 59, 60
Methuen, John, 136
Midleton, St. John Brodrick, 1st earl of, 169
Monaghan (county), 105, 167
Monck, George (later duke of Albemarle), 67, 69
Monmouth, James Scott, duke of, 39, 79
Montgomery, Hugh, 28
Mossom, Robert, bp. of Derry, 37
Mountjoy, Charles Blount, 8th Baron, 27
Munro, Robert, 32
Munster, 60, 61

North, Frederick North, Lord, 128, 129, 130, 133, 134, 138
Northern Ireland, 168
Northey, Sir Edward, 100
Northington, Robert Henley, 2nd earl of, 132–3, 134
Norway, 13, 18
Nottingham, Daniel Finch, 2nd earl of, 100, 101

O'Brien, R. B., 47
O'Connell, Daniel, 142, 143, 144, 150, 151
O'Doherty, Sir Cahir, 27
O'Donnell, Rory, earl of Tyrconnell, 29
O'Hegarty, P. S., 149
O'More, Rory, 49
O'Neill, Con, 28
O'Neill, Hugh, earl of Tyrone, 26, 27, 29
O'Neill, Sir Phelim, 52
O'Neill, Owen Roe, 32, 51, 61
O'Rahilly, T. F., 15
O'Reilly, Hugh, titular abp. of Armagh, 51
Ormond, James Butler, 12th earl and 1st duke of, 34, 35, 38, 39, 41, 42, 43, 54–6, 58, 59, 60–1, 62, 69, 70–5, 79, 80, 82
Orrery, Roger Boyle, 1st earl of, 69, 71, 72
Ossory, Thomas Butler, earl of, 72, 73, 81

Parnell, Charles Stewart, 151
Partick, St., 15
Peden, Alexander, 35, 37, 44
Pelham, Thomas, 132, 133
Phipps, Sir Constantine, 105
Pitt, William (the younger), 131, 134, 135, 136, 137, 139
Pius IX, 152
Ponsonby, William Brabazon and George, 135
Portland, William Bentinck, 3rd duke of, 130, 131, 132–3, 137, 138
Port Patrick, 30, 41
Portugal, 136
Preston, Thomas, 51
Pulteney, Daniel, 136

Ranelagh, Richard Jones, 3rd Viscount, 69, 76–8, 80
Rawdon, Sir George, 37, 41, 43
Redmond, John, 151, 163–4, 165, 166

Renwick, James, 37
Rinuccini, Giovanni Battista, 47, 62
Robartes, John Robartes, 2nd Baron, 69, 70, 73, 74, 75
Rochester, Laurence Hyde, earl of, 81
Rockingham, Charles Watson-Wentworth, 2nd marquess of, 129, 130
Rome, 61, 164
Russell, Lord John, 153
Rutland, Charles Manners, 4th duke of, 131, 133, 135, 136, 138

Scarampi, Peitro, 60, 62
Scotland, 23, 26–45 passim, 79–80, 88, 95, 102, 152, 170
Shelburne, William Petty, 2nd earl of, 129, 130, 131
Sheridan, Richard Brinsley, 136
Singleton, Henry, 121
Sligo, 61
Smith, F. E. (later 1st earl of Birkenhead), 16
Southwell, Sir Robert, 43, 81, 94, 95, 98, 100, 101
St. Andrews, 32
Stormont, 170
Swift, Jonathan, 104–5, 111–22 passim
Sydney, Thomas Townshend, 1st Viscount, 134

Talbot, Peter, titular abp. of Dublin, 74, 75
Temple, Sir John, 60
Tierney, Michael, 16
Tindal, Matthew, 114
Trench, Richard Chenevix, abp. of Dublin, 155–6
Tyrconnell, Richard Talbot, earl of, 87

Ulster, 26–45 passim, 49, 52, 53, 54, 58, 60, 61, 79, 88, 96, 104, 160–70 passim
United Irishmen, 142, 150

Vesey, John, abp. of Tuam, 105
Vigors, Bartholomew, bp. of Ferns, 94

Walker, George, 88
Walker, Patrick, 44
Walkington, Edward, bp. of Down and Connor, 93
Waterford (city), 55; (diocese), 90, 116
Wentworth, Thomas, earl of Strafford, 31, 32, 69

Wesley, John, 21
Westminster, 128, 129, 137, 153, 158, 159, 163
William III, 87, 88, 91-2, 99
Wodrow, Robert, 34
Wyche, Sir Cyril, 81

Yelverton, Barry, 127
York, 34
Young Ireland, 142, 151

P. 47